REACHING
FOR RAINBOWS

REACHING
FOR RAINBOWS

RESOURCES FOR CREATIVE WORSHIP

BY
ANN WEEMS

THE WESTMINSTER PRESS
PHILADELPHIA

Scripture quotations marked "TEV" (Today's English
Version) are from the *Good News Bible*—Old Testament: Copyright © American Bible Society 1976; New
Testament: Copyright © American Bible Society 1966,
1971, 1976.

Book Design by Dorothy Alden Smith

Published by The Westminster Press®
Philadelphia, Pennsylvania

PRINTED IN THE UNITED STATES OF AMERICA
9 8 7 6 5 4 3 2

Library of Congress Cataloging in Publication Data

Weems, Ann, 1934–
    Reaching for rainbows.

    Bibliography: p.
    1. Worship programs.   I.   Title.
BV198.W38   264'.051   80–19330
ISBN 0–664–24355–X

To Don
  who leaves rainbows in his path

CONTENTS

SERVICES OF WORSHIP

ACKNOWLEDGMENTS

The author wishes to thank the following publications, in whose pages certain of these poems and readings first appeared, for permission to include them in this book: *Presbyterian Life*— "Balloons Belong in Church," "Good News Music," "O, Lord, You Were Born!"; *A.D.*—"To You!", "I Celebrate the Church of Jesus Christ," "Our Lively Loving Lord" (retitled "The Lord of Life"); *Concern*—"An Experiment in Community" (retitled "Jesus and Dancing"), and the Benediction from "The Widow's Offering"; *Lutheran Standard*—"The Church of Jesus Christ" (retitled "Where Is the Church?").

PREFACE

In recent years many of us in the church have been agonizingly aware of ho-hum worship. The droning voices, joyless spirits, and bored expressions of uninvolved persons in the pew have caused us to wonder whether Christians really believe the news is good. Now worship is changing. Contemporary forms are appearing. This book is a result of my own searching for ways to chisel through our lukewarm worship without giving in to the temptation to innovate for innovation's sake. I celebrate the church and find much to admire in our traditional forms of worship. But it seems to me that God expects us to use our imagination and creativity to find meaningful ways of worshiping in the here and now.

My involvement began in area meetings of United Presbyterian women where we experimented with new forms of worship that we hoped would touch the women in their living. I've also spent several years on the creative worship committee in my local church, Trinity Presbyterian in St. Louis, where we have five or six "family" services of worship each year. I have written liturgy and led worship on the various judicatory levels of the United Presbyterian Church, as well as for several ecumenical services including the triennial meeting of Church Women United. I've written for various denominational magazines and have led workshops on contemporary worship locally, regionally, and, recently, at a national triennial meeting of Presbyterian women at Purdue.

What I've discovered is that the person in the pew is eager to participate, eager to celebrate the good news, eager to become "family" with other Christians in the church community, eager to praise God for the Word spoken through the life and death and resurrection of Jesus Christ.

Also I have discovered that most of us within the church *do* know what the good news is. Most of us have little trouble remembering what God has done in the past. When our worship becomes dull, when our response is rote, when our ritual lacks vitality, it is not because we have forgotten the good news; it's because we speak of the good news in the past tense. We tell the story as though it had an ending 2,000 years ago. We live our lives as though the story is over and done with. Worship that is life-giving, worship that is a real response to God's grace, tells the good news in the present tense. God not only entered history two thousand years ago, God enters now. Jesus invades our everyday world. He marches into our life-styles, our jobs, our homes, our politics, our relationships, our suffering and our joy. The amazing fact of the cross is that God entered into our godforsakenness and is with us . . . here . . . now. And when he speaks to us, it's not about stained-glass windows or one-hundred-voice choirs, as lovely as they are. When he speaks to us, it's about hunger and thirst, about light and darkness, about freedom and yearning and broken relationships, about hurting and tears wiped away. No matter how otherworldly we try to become in our worship we are brought back to the realities of this world by the sacraments. Jesus asks us to remember him, not in any ethereal way, but by the universal act of sitting down to supper, a simple meal of bread and wine. He baptizes not with costly oil but with ordinary water. He calls not just kings and clergy but people with no credentials. Jesus sits down to life with us and makes his way behind our masks and down into our being, where we are stripped of all pretense. Worship that mirrors God in our humanness is worship that is alive.

I can't separate worship from our daily living. In our worship the human and the holy must meet in relevancy, confession, festivity, and hope. Otherwise our words do not translate into loving justice, doing mercy, and walking humbly with God.

My hope is that this book will fall into the hands of those who dream dreams, those who expect miracles, those who reach for rainbows, those who hear the voice of God in their everyday.

READINGS
FOR
WORSHIP

REACHING FOR RAINBOWS

I keep reaching for rainbows . . .
Thinking one God's morning
I will wake up with rainbow ribbons in my hair,
With hurts painted over in hues that only angel wings could brush,
Black obliterated, chaos hurled beyond the rainbow and my vision,
The world created in a myriad of colors:
The hungry fed,
The dying held,
The maimed walking,
The angry stroked,
The violent calmed,
The oppressed freed,
The oppressors changed,
And every tear wiped away.
I keep reaching for rainbows,
But instead of colors in our storm,
Gray and black infiltrate, dirtying the sky,
And I hear human voices wailing in the darkness,
The never-ending darkness. . . .
Just the same
I know the promise of the rainbow.
I keep thinking I'll turn a corner one day
And find a litany of rainbows
Flung across the sky,
Hosannaing back and forth

Through all the ages and
Out into eternity forever amen!
Every tear wiped away—
It's a promise—
When we become rainbows to each other.

STATEMENT OF FAITH

We believe in God, in Jesus Christ, in the Holy Spirit, and in you
    and in me.
We believe the Holy Spirit has freed us to worship as a commu-
    nity.
We believe the Holy Spirit works through
        balloons and ministers
        daisies and wiggly children
        clanging cymbals and silence
        drama and the unexpected
        choirs and banners
        touching and praying
        spontaneity and planning
        faith and doubt
        tears and laughter
        leading and supporting
        hugging and kneeling
        dancing and stillness
        applauding and giving
        creativity and plodding
        words and listening
        holding and letting go
        thank you and help me
        Scripture and allelulas
        agonizing and celebrating
        accepting and caring

through you and through me
through Love.
We believe God's Holy Spirit lives in this community of dancing,
hand-holding people where lines of age and politics and life-
styles are crossed.
We believe in praising God for Life.
We believe in responding to God's grace and love and justice for
all people.
We believe in the poetry within each of us.
We believe in dreams and visions.
We believe in old people running and children leading.
We believe in the Kingdom of God within us.
We believe in Love.

I'D WRITE FOR YOU
A RAINBOW

If I could, I'd write for you a rainbow
And splash it with all the colors of God
And hang it in the window of your being
So that each new God's morning
Your eyes would open first
                                    to Hope and Promise.
If I could, I'd wipe away your tears
And hold you close forever in shalom.
But God never promised
I could write a rainbow,
Never promised I could suffer for you,
Only promised I could love you.
That I do.

BALLOONS BELONG
IN CHURCH

I took to church one morning a happy four-year-old boy
Holding a bright blue string to which was attached his much-loved
    orange balloon with pink stripes . . .
Certainly a thing of beauty
And, if not forever, at least a joy for a very important now.
When later he met me at the door,
Clutching blue string, orange and pink bobbing behind him,
He didn't have to tell me something had gone wrong.
"What's the matter?"
He wouldn't tell me.
"I bet they loved your balloon . . ."
Out it came then, mocking the teacher's voice:
"We don't bring balloons to church."
Then that little four-year-old, his lip a bit trembly, asked:
"Why aren't balloons allowed in church? I thought God would
    like balloons."
I celebrate balloons, parades, and chocolate chip cookies.
I celebrate seashells and elephants and lions that roar.
I celebrate roasted marshmallows and chocolate cake and fresh
    fish.
I celebrate aromas: bread baking, mincemeat, lemons . . .
I celebrate seeing: bright colors, wheat in a field, wild flowers . . .
I celebrate hearing: waves pounding, rain falling, soft voices . . .
I celebrate touching: toes in the sand, a kitten's fur, another
    person . . .

I celebrate the sun that shines slap dab in our faces . . .
I celebrate snow falling:
    the wondrous quiet of the snow falling . . .
I celebrate the crashing thunder and the brazen lightning . . .
And I celebrate the green of the world, the life-giving green, the
    hope-giving green . . .
I celebrate birth: the wonder—the miracle—of that tiny life al-
    ready asserting its selfhood.

I celebrate children
        who laugh out loud
        who walk in the mud and dawdle in the puddles
        who put chocolate fingers anywhere
        who like to be tickled
        who scribble in church
        who whisper in loud voices
        who sing in louder voices
        who run—and laugh when they fall
        who cry at the top of their lungs
        who cover themselves with Band-Aids
        who squeeze the toothpaste all over the bathroom
        who slurp their soup
        who chew cough drops
        who ask questions
        who give us sticky, paste-covered creations
        who want their pictures taken
        who don't use their napkins
        who bury their goldfish, sleep with the dog, scream at their
            best friends
        who hug us in a hurry and rush outside without their hats.
I celebrate children who are so busy living they don't have time
    for our hangups,
And I celebrate adults who are as little children.

I celebrate the person who breaks up the meaningless routines of
    life,
The person who stops to reflect, to question, to doubt,

21

the person who isn't afraid to feel,
    the person who refuses to play the game.
I celebrate anger at injustice.
I celebrate tears for the mistreated, the hurt, the lonely.
I celebrate the community that cares—the church.
I celebrate the church!
I celebrate the times when we in the church made it,
When we answered a cry,
When we held to our warm and well-fed bodies a cold and lonely
    world.
I celebrate the times when we let God get through to our hiding
    places,
  Through our maze of meetings
    our pleasant facade—
        deep down to our selfhood,
            deep down to where we really are.
  Call it heart, soul, naked self—
  It's where we hide
    deep down away from God
      and away from each other.
I celebrate the times when the church is the church,
      When we are Christians,
      When we are living, loving, contributing.
God's children—I celebrate that we are called God's children
    even when we are in hiding.
I celebrate love—the moments when the you is more important
    than the I.
I celebrate perfect love—the cross, the Christ,
    loving in spite of,
      giving without reward.
I celebrate the music within a person that must be heard.
I celebrate life—that we may live more abundantly.
Where did we get the idea that balloons don't belong in church?
Where did we get the idea that God loves gray and sh-h-h-h
And drab and anything will do?
I think it's blasphemy not to appreciate the joy in God's world.
I think it's blasphemy not to bring our joy into God's church.
For God so loved the world

That Christ hung there
Loving the unlovable.
What beautiful gift cannot be offered unto the Lord—
Whether it's a balloon or a song or some joy that sits within you
     waiting to have the lid taken off?
The Scriptures say there's a time to laugh and a time to weep.
It's not hard to see the reasons for crying in a world where hatred
     for others is so manifest;
But it's also not hard to see the reasons for laughter in a world
     where God's love is so manifest.
So celebrate!
Bring your balloons and your butterflies, your bouquets of flowers,
Bring the torches and hold them high!
Dance your dances, paint your feelings, sing your songs, whistle,
     laugh.
Life is a celebration, an affirmation of God's love.
Life is distributing more balloons.
For God so loved the world . . .
Surely that's a cause for joy.
Surely we should celebrate!
Good news! That God should love us that much.
Where did we ever get the idea that balloons don't belong in
     church?

GOOD NEWS MUSIC

How long will we come before the Lord
    with tired spirits and droning voices?
How long will we sit in half-filled churches
    and sing praise with noiseless songs?
How long will we worship with bored faces and dulled senses
    and offer tin when we could give gold?
Do we or do we not believe the news is good?

O Lord, you love us!
    Why aren't we shouting?
We don't have to earn it!
    Why aren't we singing?
The stone's rolled away!
    Why aren't we dancing
        to your good news music?

O Lord, you love us!
    Why aren't the bells pealing?
The victory's won!
    Why aren't the drums beating?
And you forgave us!
    Why aren't the harps resounding
        to your good news music?
Why aren't the feet stomping
    and the doves flying
        and the bands marching

and the fingers snapping
and the tongues praising
and the hands clapping
and the trumpets blaring
and the choirs singing
and the cymbals clashing
and the children
laughing?

And why aren't the people
coming
to
bow
down?

Why aren't the eyes smiling
and the knees kneeling
and the banners blowing
and the horns sounding
and the voices calling
and the crowds clamoring
and the arms waving
and the tambourines playing
and the hearts humming
and the old men
running?

And why aren't we
crowning
Christ
Lord
of
Lords?

If the news is good . . .
Sing!

THE LORD OF LIFE

O Lord, we're playing Pharisee again,
  More interested in the Sunday morning count
   Than in the feeding of your sheep,
  More interested in stars for our crowns
   Than in that cup of cold water,
  More interested in tradition and appearance
   Than in the following of our Lord.

O Jesus, you were real
And we made you saccharine and
  hung you on the church school wall
And told all the little children
  you wanted them to sit still.
O Jesus, you were here and now
And we made you something in the sweet by and by
And told all the people in need
  to see you in heaven.
O Jesus, you walked in our shoes in our marketplace
And we told you to stay in your sandals,
In a faraway place, in a long ago time,
  Stay back in the Bible.
O Jesus, we made you a baby that didn't cry,
  We made you a boy with good manners,
  We made you a man, sweet and gentle.
  We tossed you pennies,
  Then told you how to spend them.

We built you temples,
Then told you who could enter them.
We made you wood and plastic and concrete
And locked you in the church.
We made you a goody-goody god
And stood before the world with joyless faces
        and pointing fingers
            and tsk-tsk-tsk cold voices,
                declaring thou-shalt-nots.
O Lord! We paid no attention to Who You Are: the Lord of Life!

Jesus was into life
    in such a way
That you either had to follow him
    or resent his attempt to bring you change.
That's still who he is:
    Someone who's going to make you see yourself
        if you have ears to hear.
O Lord, we're playing Pharisee again,
Playing at church
And making excuses about the real thing:
    Not me,
    Not now,
    Not with my income,
    Not with all I have to do . . .
Or making after-all speeches:
    After all, I give more than others I could name;
    After all, I do have five children;
    After all, I haven't been feeling well . . .
Or putting God off:
    As soon as we get the house paid for,
    As soon as we get the kids through college,
    As soon as we get this painting finished . . .
Christ was crucified for saying, Follow me now.
He was crucified for saying:
    You're storing up treasures
    Feed my sheep!
    You're blasphemers!

Love God with everything you've got!
And don't forget that cup of cold water.
Sweet and gentle? Meek and mild?
Christ came treading into our marketplaces, our temples, our
    homes—even into our private person—
    Teaching in the temple
    Preaching by the sea
    Questioning religious customs
    Breaking the ceremonial law
    Righting injustices
    Healing the sick
    Being joyful in the company of friends
    Calling the children
    Chiding good church members
    Caring for unimportant people
    Seeking out the sinners.
Christ came humbling himself,
Came loving the poor, the hungry, the lonely.
Christ came loving—
    This Lord of Life,
        This living, loving Lord.
O Lord, open our eyes to see the Pharisee within us.
Open our ears that we might hear the prophecy
Of the possibility of change.
Open the church doors that we might follow
    Our living, loving Lord
        Out into the marketplace.

CHRISTMAS TREES
AND STRAWBERRY SUMMERS

What I'd really like is a life of Christmas trees and strawberry
    summers,
A walk through the zoo with a pocketful of bubble gum and a
    string of balloons.
I'd say "yes" to blueberry mornings and carefree days with rain-
    bow endings.
I'd keep the world in springtime and the morning glories bloom-
    ing,
But life is more than birthday parties;
Life is more than candied apples.

I'd rather hear the singing than the weeping.
I'd rather see the healing than the violence.
I'd rather feel the pleasure than the pain.
I'd rather know security than fear.
I'd like to keep the cotton candy coming,
But life is more than fingers crossed;
Life is more than wishing.

Christ said, "Follow me."
And, of course, I'd rather not.
I'd rather pretend that doesn't include me.
I'd rather sit by the fire and make my excuses.
I'd rather look the other way,
Not answer the phone,
And be much too busy to read the paper.

But I said YES and
That means risk—
It means here I am, ready or not!

O Christmas trees and strawberry summers,
You're what I like and you are real,
But so are hunger
    and misery
        and hate-filled red faces.
So is confrontation.
So is injustice.
Discipleship means sometimes it's going to rain in my face.

But when you've been blind and now you see . . .
When you've been deaf and now you hear . . .
When you've never understood and now you know . . .
Once you know who God calls you to be,
You're not content with sitting in corners.
There's got to be some alleluia shouting,
    Some speaking out
    Some standing up
    Some caring
    Some sharing
    Some community
    Some risk.
Discipleship means living what you know.
Discipleship means "Thank you, Lord"
For Christmas trees and strawberry summers
And even for rain in my face.

TO YOU!

This morning I was toasted by a two-year-old
Who raised her orange juice glass to mine and said, "To you!"
She brought the morning; she moved a mountain;
She brought flowers out of barren land and sunlight from darkness.
What a way to start the day—affirmed and celebrated!

Remember to celebrate those across the breakfast table.
When did you last tell them they are precious?
You told them to take out the trash, to make their beds,
But did you tell them they are cherished?
You told them they were wrong; you told them to hurry up;
But did you tell them they are beautiful?
We celebrate events or days or heroes,
But take for granted the joy of the familiar.

So here's to you, familiar faces at my breakfast table!
Here's to smiles, sleepy kisses, and theological questions at dawn!
Here's to unbrushed teeth, unmade beds, and unpicked-up
    clothes!
Here's to dirty tennis shoes with one blue sock and one brown!
Here's to last night's scores and news told before I read it!
Here's to my cold cup of coffee, to the lunch forgotten!
Here's to the little girl who wants ice cream with her eggs!
Here's to the daddy who thinks that's funny!
Here's to the man who loves us so and lets us know!

I cherish you who breakfast with me.
You are sun in my rain—sustenance and star.

O Lord, free us to thank God for each other!
Free us to click orange juice glasses clear across your Kingdom
In every family and in the larger family of the gathered church.
Here's to you, saints who remembered to love!
Here's to those who heal, teach, listen, comfort;
Who feed the hungry, clothe the naked, give a cup of cold water,
Weep with those who weep, rejoice with those who rejoice,
And stand by to pick us up and brush us off!
Here's to the peacemakers and the prophets—
Their justice, their mercy, their humility,
Their strength that does not falter!
Here's to those who have been freed to free us,
To their song that never ends,
To the saints who keep on dancing!
Here's to you!

GREENLESS CHILD

I watched her go uncelebrated into the second grade,
A greenless child,
Gray among the orange and yellow,
Attached too much to corners and to other people's sunshine.
She colors the rainbow brown
And leaves balloons unopened in their packages.
Oh, who will touch this greenless child?
Who will plant alleluias in her heart
And send her dancing into all the colors of God?
Or will she be left like an unwrapped package on the kitchen
    table—
Too dull for anyone to take the trouble?
Does God think we're her keeper?

GIFT OF GOD

Gift of God
You
  sit next to me and
                 pass me Bread and Wine . . .
You
  always there
         with communion in your countenance
 reaching ready
         aware accepting affirming

Gift of God
You
  touch this lepered me
              to wholeness

Instrument of God
You
  hear alleluias through obscenities
    see rainbows in the darkest storms
      unearth flowers in the snow

Gift of God
I thank God for you!

TOUCH IN CHURCH

What is all this touching in church?
It used to be a person could come to church and sit in the pew
  and not be bothered by all this friendliness and
    certainly not by touching.
I used to come to church and leave untouched.
Now I have to be nervous about what's expected of me.
I have to worry about responding to the person sitting next to me.
Oh, I wish it could be the way it used to be;
I could just ask the person next to me: How are you?
And the person could answer: Oh, just fine,
And we'd both go home ... strangers who have known each other
  for twenty years.
But now the minister asks us to look at each other.
I'm worried about that hurt look I saw in that woman's eyes.
Now I'm concerned, because when the minister asks us to pass the
  peace,
The man next to me held my hand so tightly I wondered if he had
  been touched in years.
Now I'm upset because the lady next to me cried and then apolo-
  gized
And said it was because I was so kind and that she needed
A friend right now.
Now I have to get involved.
Now I have to suffer when this community suffers.
Now I have to be more than a person coming to observe a service.

That man last week told me I'd never know how much I'd touched
his life.
All I did was smile and tell him I understood what it was to be
lonely.
Lord, I'm not big enough to touch and be touched!
The stretching scares me.
What if I disappoint somebody?
What if I'm too pushy?
What if I cling too much?
What if somebody ignores me?
"Pass the peace."
"The peace of God be with you." "And with you."
And mean it.
Lord, I can't resist meaning it!
I'm touched by it, I'm enveloped by it!
I find I do care about that person next to me!
I find I *am* involved!
And I'm scared.
O Lord, be here beside me.
You touch me, Lord, so that I can touch and be touched!
So that I can care and be cared for!
So that I can share my life with all those others that belong to you!
All this touching in church—Lord, it's changing me!

TO TOM McCALL,
WHEREVER YOU ARE

A few years ago there was a little boy in my church school class who was perpetual motion. He never sat down and the teachers could not guess what he would do next. He moved away and I've lost track of the family, but I've always had a soft spot in my heart for Tom.

Reader:
> I've always loved you, Tom McCall,
> Of spirit large and figure small,
> Since first we met in the church's hall
> And you stuck your tongue out, Tom McCall.

Individual Voices
> 1: Tom McCall, all legs and feet,
> 2: Tom McCall never sits on the seat.
> 3: Tom McCall, your shirttail's out.
> 1: Tom McCall, do you always shout?
> 2: Tom McCall, paint on your face,
> 3: Did you have to paint the rest of the place?

Reader:
> The choir children are in single file,
> Looking angelic all the while.
> Here comes one with a great big smile:
> Tom is backing down the aisle.

1: Tom, your choir robe's askew.
2: Tom, did it ever occur to you,
3: If you don't watch out you're gonna fall . . .
1: Now you've done it, Tom McCall!
2: Tom McCall, grin on your face,
3: You've melted hearts all over the place!

Reader:
And then in church school late in fall,
We spoke of a child who had nothing at all.
Tom took his feet from the church school wall,
Emptied his pockets and gave his all.
Here's to you, dear Tom McCall!

1: Tom McCall, all legs and feet,
2: Tom McCall never sits on the seat.
3: Tom McCall, your shirttail's out.
1: Tom McCall, do you always shout?
2: Tom McCall, paint on your face,

Reader:
Tom McCall, child of grace.

COUGH DROPS IN CHURCH

(A dialogue for parent and child)

Parent: What do you like best about church?
Child: I like cough drops.
Parent: I know you like cough drops, but what do you like best about church?
Child: Well, cough drops are important to little kids like me.
Parent: Cough drops are very nice if you have a cough.
Child: You mean if I don't have a cough, they're not nice?
Parent: Oh, I imagine you'd like them anytime, but they're for a cough.
Child: Well, I like them in church.
Parent: Cough or not?
Child: I feel so good while I'm sitting next to you and kind of snuggling up, chewing a cough drop.
Parent: Kind of good?
Child: Warm—like belonging, you know.
Parent: Belonging?
Child: That's the way I feel about church. I belong here, where the music is and where the words say that God loves me even if I am a little kid.
Parent: Even if?
Child: Well, I don't have a job or anything like that, but God doesn't seem to mind.

Parent: No, God doesn't seem to mind at all. In fact, I'd venture to say that God likes very much to have you in church, unemployed though you might be.

Child: Cough drops and all?

Parent: Cough drops and all!

HAPPY BIRTHDAY, CHURCH!

There was once a church that had only party rooms: the Session's Party Room, the Music Party Room, the Feasting Party Room, the Do Justice Party Room, the Love Mercy Party Room, the Touch Lepers Party Room. In the center of the building was a large round room with an altar and a cross: God's Party Room.

There was in the church an air of festivity and brightness that could not be denied. The people outside the church pointed their fingers and shook their heads: "Something should be done about that church." They were especially upset when they saw that the members wore party hats and smiles both inside and outside the church.

Other congregations came to take a look and were shocked when they saw this church having so much fun during a worship service, snapping their fingers and dancing.

"Sacrilegious," screamed the crowd. But the people in the church just smiled at them and went right on doing things like taking people in wheelchairs to the park and playing ball with them.

When everybody else was collecting canned goods for the poor, this church bought pizza and marched right into dingy, dirty, paint-peeling apartments and sat down to eat with the tenants.

They held picnics for the old folks home, and old men ran races while the congregation stamped their feet in applause. It was at one of these picnics that some of the members climbed up on the roof and shouted: "Good news!"

"Now we can get them for disturbing the peace," said one of the outsiders. The police arrived with sirens, ready for the arrest, and came out two hours later wearing party hats and smiles.

One Sunday afternoon, the entire congregation met at the jail and passed out flowers to the prisoners. The following week after bread and wine and much laughter at the Lord's table, the people went to the hospital and asked to see the dying patients. They held their hands and mopped their brows and spoke to them of life.

"Disgraceful!" shouted the crowd. "They must be stopped." So the crowd appealed to the governing body of the denomination, and this committee of respected church people went to see for themselves.

"Do you deny the charges of heresy?" asked the committee. "Do you deny that you've mocked the church and the Lord?" The people of the church looked into the stern red faces and smiled at them. They held out their hands to the committee and led them to the Birthday Cake Party Room. There on a table sat a large cake decorated beautifully in doves descending and red flames and words that read: HAPPY BIRTHDAY, CHURCH! The people began cutting cake and blowing up balloons and handing out party hats to the committee members.

"Wait! Wait!" cried the chairperson. "Can't you take anything seriously?"

"Yes," said the people. "We take our commitment to the Lord very seriously indeed."

"You don't take it seriously at all," interrupted the chairperson in loud voice and red face. "You have parties and wear silly hats and blow up balloons and sing and dance and have fun. Do you call that commitment?"

The people smiled at the chairperson and asked him if he'd like a glass of wine. The chairperson hit his fist on the table. "I don't want wine, and I don't want birthday cake. We're here to reprimand you. We're here to show you that you're wrong. Can't you be serious?"

"We are," said the people. "We're asking you to take communion with us."

"With birthday cake?" screamed the chairperson. "Outrageous!"

"Outrageous? We ask you to sit at our table and sup with us. God gave the Holy Spirit to believers, and that is something to celebrate! It's an occasion for a party. We are celebrants of the gift of Life. We are community. We are God's church. Why are your faces red when we are trying to do justice and love mercy? Why do you shake your fists at us when we are trying to discover the hurting and begin the healing? We are overjoyed that we can be the church, a community of people, who are many, yet one— who are different, but who walk together and welcome any who would walk with us. When we weep there is someone to weep with us and to affirm us and to take us to a party. When we see injustices, we must be about God's business of freeing the oppressed. When we are faithless, we have God's promise of forgiveness. Isn't it remarkable that we can be God's good news? Is it any wonder we have a church full of party rooms? There is so much love to celebrate!"

The committee stared at the people, and the people moved closer to them and put their arms around them. The committee chairperson stepped up to the table and sliced a piece of birthday cake, took a bite, and laughed out loud. He began slicing and passing it out.

When the wine was poured and the hands were held, the chairperson raised his glass and said: "There is so much Love to celebrate! Happy Birthday, Church!"

A GROUP OF BELIEVERS

(A reading that can be done by one person, two, three, or four. It is divided here for four readers.)

First: A group of believers gathered in a church.

Second: They believed in one God, God Almighty, who made the world and everything in it.

Third: They believed in God the Creator.
And they believed that God the Creator sent the Son, Jesus Christ, to save the world.

Fourth: They believed these things and they said them every Sunday at eleven o'clock.

Third: They were very busy and did the things most churches do.
They had church dinners and they inquired about each other's families.

First: And they read the Bible and they sent a check to missions every year,
And at Thanksgiving they collected canned goods for the poor.

Fourth: And on Sunday mornings things were done decently and in order.

All: They were good church people.

Second: But one Sunday morning during the service of worship, a little boy came running in the church door, ran right down the center aisle, and stood under the cross screaming, "Help me!"

44

Third: He was a thin child with dark, sunken eyes. The clothes
           he wore were no more than rags.
First: His feet were bare and he shivered and then, with a cry,
           fell—under the cross.
           Everything was quiet—and then a voice yelled:
Second: Get him out of here!
First: And another said:
Fourth: We don't want to get involved with his kind.
First: And a third said:
Third: Get someone else.
First: But the rest of the congregation arose quietly, in uni-
           son, and walked as if they were in step until they,
           too, stood under the cross. They bent and lifted
           the child gently and ministered unto him.
Third: And then, as if for the first time, they noticed each
           other.
           They smiled and their hands reached out to one an-
           other and they began to dance.
First: Some people laughed, and said:
Fourth: They're drunk!
First: But others asked:
Third: What does this mean?
First: And the people answered:
Second: The Lord's Spirit has been poured out upon us. The
           Lord has anointed us to care for God's children
           everywhere who are crying, "Help me!"
First: And now this church is decorated in the bright colors
           of joy. The people wear robes of caring and com-
           mitment.
Third: The call to worship is: "Help them!"
Fourth: The entire congregation dances together.

SILVER SPOONS

Reader: Once upon a time,
Chorus: Once upon a time,
Reader: There was born a beautiful baby with a silver spoon in her mouth.
Chorus: A silver spoon in her mouth.
Reader: As she grew older she realized that she could have anything she wanted—
Chorus: Servants, fine clothes, jewels, cars . . .
Reader: She married a fine man who had also been born with a silver spoon in *his* mouth—
Chorus: Anything he wanted.
Reader: Soon children were born to them and they were born . . .
Chorus: Yes, we know, with silver spoons in *their* mouths.
Reader: Anyway, one day the Lord appeared to the woman and asked, "Are you having a good life?"
Woman: "Yes,"
Reader: Said the woman,
Woman: "Very nice."
Reader: "Well," said the Lord, "I thought I would have heard from you by now."
The woman looked around to see if the Lord was talking to someone else and then, seeing no one, she answered,
Woman: "Do I know you?"

Reader:	"Well," said the Lord, "we did meet years ago, but you seem to have forgotten me."
Chorus:	The woman looked at the Lord blankly. She had no idea where they had met.
Reader:	The Lord continued: "What you have—all of your blessings, your material wealth as well as your family and friends, your beautiful life-style, the trees, the flowers, the food you eat—all came from me."
Woman:	"Oh, no!"
Chorus:	Said the woman.
Woman:	"I was born with a silver spoon in my mouth. You gave me nothing."
Reader:	"Nothing?" asked the Lord.
Woman:	"Nothing,"
Reader:	Said the woman.
Chorus:	Nothing.
Reader:	"I thought," said the Lord, "that since you have so much you might be thankful and in your gratitude you might want to share with others."
Woman:	"Oh, I see. Well, if you are a beggar, you may go to the back door and the cook will give you a plate of food."
Chorus:	*If* you chop the wood!
Reader:	"I am not a beggar," said the Lord. "I am a King."
Woman:	"Oh, well—kings may go in the front door."
Chorus:	Oh, yes, please, the front door.
Woman:	"But, if you are a king, why are you asking for a handout?"
Reader:	"It's not for me," said the king. "It's for your sisters and brothers."
Woman:	"Now I know you mistake me. I have no sisters and brothers."
Reader:	"Oh, yes," said the Lord. "You have a world full of them."
Woman:	"You mean I am to feed the world?"
Reader:	"Feed my sheep."

Woman:	"But what do you mean?"
Reader:	"You know what I mean: To whom much is given, from them much is required."
Chorus:	Much is required!
Reader:	And what happened to the woman who was born with a silver spoon in her mouth?
Chorus:	She *did* know what the Lord meant.
Reader:	And now she takes her silver spoon and feeds her hungry brothers and sisters.
	How many of you have a silver spoon?
Chorus:	What do you mean?
Reader:	You know what I mean.

COME TO THE EASTER PARTY

I think on Easter morning we should throw confetti in church!
No?
What about a little fanfare?
A deafening drum roll?
A three-minute standing ovation?
What? Have we had the drums beaten out of us
That we in the celebrative community can't really
        Get excited
                About God's aliveness?
About God's love given to us unconditionally?
Have we given Easter to the lily bearers, the bunny rabbits, the
    patent leather shoes?
Let's face it:
We live as though we don't believe in Easter.

We're the crowd—
Easily swayed,
Easily scared,
Easily calling for blood.
We're the good church people
Who can't believe Jesus meant love one another—
Not all the one anothers,
Not drug addicts and criminals.
We hate injustice when it's injustice toward us;
We love mercy when it's mercy for us;
We walk humbly with our God when it's convenient.

49

We're Babe Believers who resist the resurrection;
We're Christmas Christians who are very good at
Celebrating Christ's birth.
We can cling to the Babe.
We're even Crucifixion Christians,
Agonizing, sympathizing,
Relating to the Hero of the Cross.
We can rock a Baby;
We can weep for a Dead Man;
But what can we do with a 33-year-old who won't let the story
    end?
Easter scares us
Because we're the people who can't believe
That God gives us abundant Life;
We think we have to earn it.
In our pull-yourself-up-by-your-own-bootstraps society
It's hard to remember that God doesn't buy the self-made man.
So we in the church spend our lives showing God
What good people we are,
What achievers we are,
How much we deserve God's love.
We want to pay our own way,
But Easter says it's already been paid!
Easter says, no matter how prodigal,
We can go home again!
So come to the Easter party!
Let's celebrate that amazing grace
That in Christ's resurrection
We are still loved even at our most outrageous.
The Lord has given us the music;
All we need do is dance it!
Come to the Easter party!

YOU—SITTING IN THE PEW
NEXT TO ME

(This is a dialogue taking place between two people sitting next to each other in church. They do not look at each other, but look out over the congregation, for the dialogue is in their thoughts only—until the very end when the service is over.)

First Person:

You—sitting in the pew next to me—
I don't know you.
Oh, I know your name.
I know the "Hi, how are you?" part of you.
I know the "Rainy weather we're having, isn't it?" part of
    you.
But I don't know you—
Not what you're thinking,
Not where you've come from,
Not where you're going.
You sit so still:
Are you serene
Or are you simmering inside?
Are you content with life
Or are you churning?
Are you here because it's a habit
Or because it's a joy
Or because your mother brought you years ago?
Is it expected of you?
Are you setting an example for the children?

Are you glad to be here
Or are you just tired?
Are you bored
Or are you filled with fire?
Are you tuned into what's being said
Or are you disenchanted?
Did you come from a chaotic morning
Or from too much quiet?
Are you thinking about last night's party
Or this afternoon's ball game?
Or are you wondering what it's all about?
Will you ever reveal yourself to me
Or are you just another person in the pew I'll never know?

Second Person:
You—sitting in the pew next to me—
I don't know you.
Oh, I know your background.
I know you're here every Sunday.
I know you're very big around here—
Church school teacher, chairperson of this and that,
On all the important committees.
Even went to the national meeting, didn't you?
Who are you behind that smile,
Behind all that activity—
Are you for real?
Are you doing it all for your image
Or do you love Christ so much you've got to give your time?
Are you hustling
Or are you filled with God's spirit?
Are you desperately trying to fill the emptiness in your life
Or are you overflowing with goodwill?
Would you tell me if I asked you
Or would you play a game with me?
Would you really care if I told you my problems?
Would you really listen
Or would you be looking over my shoulder?
Could I be honest with you

Or would my honesty make you nervous?
Would you take the time?
Would you be interested to know what I feel?
Would my doubts make you uneasy?
Would you want to get involved?
Do you even care what I'm all about?
Where I'm heading,
What I'm thinking . . .
Does the fact that we're sitting side by side in God's sanctu-
    ary
Make us community?
Does it make the difference?
Or are you just another person in the pew I'll never know?

First Person:
    You—sitting in the pew next to me—
    I'm lonely.
    You'd be surprised at that, wouldn't you?
    How could I be lonely with all the family and friends I have?
    I'm not lonesome, I'm lonely!
    I'm lonely deep down where it hurts.
    I want to reach out to somebody and say:
    This is me. This is really me.
    But everybody passes quickly.
    They're all so busy.
    Everything's kept superficial
    As if when we busy ourselves with enough things
    We won't have to think;
    We won't have to face our emotions.
    Oh, I long to cut through our rote responses, our pleasantries,
        our right answers.
    I want to say: I'm sorry you have a cold, and I'm glad we're
        having weather,
    But what are you doing inside there?
    What kind of a somersault is going on deep inside of you?
    Are you angry?
    Are you hurt?
    Are you frightened?

Are you confused?
Are you who you want to be?
I'd be interested in what you feel
Would you be interested in what I feel?
What I'm searching for,
                hoping for,
                        reaching for?
It's all a part of what I think it means to be here,
In God's church.
Are you lonely, too?
Do you wonder or do you have it all solved?
Or do you even care?
Are you just another person in the pew I'll never know?

Second Person:
You—sitting in the pew next to me—
I'm scared.
Years are passing quickly
And I seem to have little control over my life.
It's as though somebody else
Set out a course for me.
When did I decide on this life-style?
I'm scared by the subtleties of life.
I'm scared by what's expected of me
By some unknown "they" out there.
I'm scared by the pushing, the pulling, the pressures.
Whoever decided that I had to live on this street in this house
And work like crazy to live on another street in a bigger
        house?
Whoever decided for me that success was chasing after
        things?
And that there's no end to it . . .
Keep chasing . . .
My life dedicated to owning.
Whoever decided I owed my children bigger and better
        things?
I'm scared when I take a good look at my way of life.

I'm scared when I look at myself.
That's why I'm here—
Because I've heard there is a better way.
I've heard that some people take Christ seriously.
I've heard that maybe in church I could be born again. find new life
Is it possible?
Could I talk to you about it?
Would you laugh to think successful me needs you?
Or would you be compassionate because you know I'm
    scared?
Maybe you'll be the one to tell me . . .
Or are you just another person in the pew I'll never know?

First Person:
    You—sitting in the pew next to me—
    What are you really doing here?
    Do you believe in Christ Jesus?
    How much?
    Enough to risk?
    How much of a risk?
    Risk your reputation?
    Risk your family?
    Your money?
    Do you?
    Do you believe in Christ?
    Or is Christianity a convenience?
    Something to fill in on consensus forms,
    Something one just goes along with,
    Something undemanding,
    Something nice . . .
    Do you believe?
    Do you know what you believe?
    Will you share it with me?
    Or are you just another person in the pew I'll never know?

*(At this point, the two persons come out of their thoughts. The
service is over. One turns to the other and says:)*

Second Person:
    Hi, how are you?

First Person:
    Oh, fine. Rainy weather we're having, isn't it?

Second Person:
    Yes, isn't it?

I CELEBRATE THE CHURCH
OF JESUS CHRIST

I celebrate the church of Jesus Christ,
where two or three or thousands can gather together
in the Lord's name
and touch this world
    with the amazing good news that somebody cares,
    that God joins us in community so that someday
    this world will be loved to wholeness.

I celebrate this community,
where the people say Yes in the face of No,
where they light candles in the darkest night,
where healing and compassion leave no time for self-righteousness,
and the life-sustaining love of Christ is evident in the life of the
    believers.

I celebrate the church, where we dare to stand up,
where risk runs rampant,
and you and I and all Christ's disciples
are called upon to follow
    even when it costs us something,
      something precious
    like our friends,
      like our respectability,
        like our future with the company.

I celebrate the church, where we are called
　　from half-heartedness to commitment:
commitment to a God who calls us to change,
　　　to change our direction,
　　　　to be reborn
　　　　　to a way of life where others are significant.

I celebrate the church,
where every child of God is hailed as unique and valuable,
where arms are opened to the world's outcasts,
where the tired, beaten, disillusioned world is invited in
　　and surprised
　　　by the life-giving word
　　　　that Christ accepts the children,
　　　　　all the children of the world.

I celebrate the injustices righted,
　　the protests made on behalf of the battered.
I celebrate the awareness and awakening to humanity's suffering,
　　the pain alleviated,
　　　the scars erased.
I celebrate the mercy and forgiveness
　　the tears wiped away,
　　　the hands held,
　　　　the gifts given,
　　　　　the children treasured and nurtured,
　　　　　the races won,
　　　　　the failures met.
I celebrate the healthy grieving for lost children.
I celebrate the life-enhancing hope that brings
　　the piecing together of the scattered.
I celebrate the celebrants.
I celebrate the church of Jesus Christ,
　　whose supportive community
　　　holds me when I'm tempted to give up,
　　　enfolds me when I'm hurting,

affirms me, reaches out to me,
    gives to me, receives from me.

I cannot live abundantly without this community, God's church,
where turning to one another and working and rejoicing with one
    another is a way of life—
A Way of life God chose for us,
    a gift God gave us,
        a mission that we share;
a mission that cuts across barriers,
    racial and cultural,
        national and international;
a mission that unites local and regional,
    men and women,
        young and old.
I celebrate this way of life
that takes me and mine from the center of things
    and focuses on ours and theirs.
I celebrate the trust we hold,
    the spirit we share,
        the attitude of partnership.
I celebrate that love lives among us,
    that God's spirit pervades our being, our community.
I see God's face within the lives of these celebrants.
I hear God's voice in the vision of men and women who call us
    to a better way,
        a higher hope.
For God works miracles in common clay pots,
Changing caterpillars to butterflies and water to wine,
Changing seeds to oak trees and night to day,
Changing winter to springtime,
Changing lives from ordinary to abundant.
We as God's celebrants dance through this world together
    listening for God's music,
    responding to God's word,
    praising God with clapping hands and moving feet,
    praising God with justice and mercy and humbleness,
    praising God with changed lives.

Let's celebrate the church of Jesus Christ
where the wonderful wildness of God
breaks through common clay pots
and fills us with a holy spirit that overflows
and we see rainbows,
many-splendored colors,
light in pitch darkness—
and every day is a festival of faith!

LORD OF THE DANCE

(This reading has been used in worship services with the hymn "I Danced in the Morning," by Sydney Carter, set to an old Shaker tune arranged and adapted by him. "Dance" translates as "Life.")

When they ask what happened here,
We'll simply say
Christ came by and we learned his dance.

The Lord does his dance on the temple floor
And the Pharisees are properly shocked:
A mad man,
Dangerous,
Unfit to guide our youth,
A heretic!
And they flee to the public
Where their praying can be seen.

The Lord does his dance with a tax collector
And the Sadducees scream: Now!
Now do you see who he is? He dines with sinners
While we we have all this work to do.
The man's a winebibber!

The Lord does his dance with a woman of the streets
And the church people rub their hands together gleefully.
Aha! Now we've got you!

But he looked into them
And they crept away,
Unable to throw the first stone.

The Lord does his dance with all the wrong people:
With slaves and lepers and tax collectors,
With cursing fishermen and adulterers and thieves,
With outcasts and castoffs.
He dances with the unclean, with the orphan, with the displaced,
    with the unwhole.
And he won't dance with us,
No matter how plaintively we call
Lord, Lord . . .
He won't dance with us
Until we become
(Of all things)
As little children;
Until we admit we are the needy,
    we are the outcasts,
    we are the orphans.
Then he says to us:
    Come unto me!
    And we become the accepted unacceptables,
    Our brokenness is bound,
    And we are able to follow the dance.
The music is never-ending
And if we miss a step or two,
Or if we fall exhausted,
The Lord is always there to pull us to our feet.

So come now, let's dance in the temple!
Let's dance in the city!
Let's dance in the sanctuary and in the streets!
Let's join hands and dance where
The music leads us,
For the Lord's dance is never ending;
The music goes on forever!

A LITANY
OF CREATION AND FAITH

Minister: In times to come, your children will ask you:
"Why did the Lord our God ask us to obey these laws?"

People: We will tell our children:
Once we were slave people
And now we are free.
Once we were no people
And now we are God's people.

Minister: On that first morning
God called us.

People: God called us from nothing.

Minister: Out of nothing came being.

People: Out of darkness came light.

Minister: Out of chaos came order.

People: Out of nothing came life.

Minister: On that first morning God called us.

People: This morning God calls us
To be the people of faith in the midst
Of meaninglessness.

Minister: In the midst of meaninglessness

People: God calls us to meaning.

Minister: Out of brokenness

People: God calls us to wholeness.

Minister: Out of divisiveness

People: God calls us to community.

Minister:	Out of tears
People:	God calls us to laughter.
Minister:	Out of self-centeredness
People:	God calls us to love one another.
Minister:	Out of unfaithfulness
People:	God calls us to faith.
Minister:	Out of death
People:	God calls us to life.
Minister:	And we will say to our children:
People:	Come with us and worship God,
	Who has created and is creating in our midst.
	Come with us and keep covenant.
Minister:	In times to come
	We will tell our children:
People:	Once we were slaves
	But now we are free;
	Once we were no people
	But now we are God's people.
Minister:	Out of death to resurrection,
	Out of chaos to rebirth,
	Out of unfaithfulness to faith—
People:	Praise God for these wondrous gifts!

GIFTS FROM GOD

The steadfast love of the Lord never ceases;
God's mercies never come to an end.
They are new every morning.

The Lord God gave the peoples of the earth a garden,
And the people said: "That's very nice, God, but that's not
    enough. We'd like a little knowledge, please."
The Lord God gave them knowledge,
And the people said: "Now that we have knowledge, we'd like
    things."
The Lord God gave the people things,
But they always said: "That's not quite enough."
So the Lord God gave them gifts unequaled:
    The Sun
    Lightning and Thunder
    Rain and Flowers
    Animals and Birds and Fish
    Trees and Stars and the Moon
God gave them the Rainbow
God parted the Red Sea and gave them Manna
God gave them Prophets
    And Children
    And Each Other,
But still the people said, "That's not quite enough."
God loved the people,
And out of ultimate merciful goodness

God gave them the Gift of Gifts—
A Christmas present never to be forgotten—
God gave them Love
In the form of God's Son,
    Even Christ Jesus.

There are some that don't open their eyes or their ears or their
    hearts
And they still say, that's not quite enough.
They wander through the stores looking for Christmas;
But others open their whole being to the Lord,
    Bending their knees to praise God,
        Carrying Christmas with them every day.
For these the whole world is a gift!

CHRISTMAS COMES

Christmas comes every time we see God in other persons.
The human and the holy meet in Bethlehem
                                    or in Times Square,
For Christmas comes like a golden storm on its way
    to Jerusalem—
    Determinedly, inevitably . . .
Even now it comes
In the face of hatred and warring—
No atrocity too terrible to stop it,
No Herod strong enough,
No hurt deep enough,
No curse shocking enough,
No disaster shattering enough—
        For someone on earth will see the star,
        Someone will hear the angel voices,
        Someone will run to Bethlehem,
        Someone will know peace and goodwill:
        The Christ will be born!

PEACE ON EARTH

"Peace on earth, goodwill to all" . . .
The song came out like one loud hosanna
Hurled through the earth's darkness,
Lighting the Bethlehem sky.
Sometimes I hear it now,
But it means a baby in a manger;
It means a time of year,
A cozy feeling,
A few coins in the Salvation Army bucket.
It doesn't mean much—
And then it's gone,
Lost in the tinsel.

Where did the angels' song go?
Who hushed the alleluias?
Was it death and war and disease and poverty?
Was it darkness and chaos and famine and plague?
Who brought violence and took away the sweet plucking of heav-
     enly harps?
Who brought despair and took away hope?
Who brought barrenness and crushed the flowers?
Who stole the music and brought the silence?
What Herods lurk within our world seeking to kill our children?
Are there still those
Who listen for the brush of angel wings
And look for stars above some godforsaken little stable?

Are there still those
Who long to hear an angel's song
And touch a star?
To kneel beside some other shepherd
In the hope of catching a glimpse of eternity in a baby's smile?
Are there still those who sing
"Peace on earth, goodwill to all"?
If there are—then, O Lord,
Keep ablaze their flickering candle
In the darkness of this world!

THE CROSS
IN THE MANGER

If there is no cross in the manger,
    there is no Christmas.
If the Babe doesn't become the Adult,
    there is no Bethlehem star.
If there is no commitment in us,
    there are no wise men searching.
If we offer no cup of cold water,
    there is no gold, no frankincense, no myrrh.
If there is no praising God's name,
    there are no angels singing.
If there is no spirit of alleluia,
    there are no shepherds watching.
If there is no standing up, no speaking out, no risk,
    there is no Herod, no flight into Egypt.
If there is no room in our inn,
    then "Merry Christmas" mocks the Christ Child,
    and the Holy Family is just a holiday card,
    and God will loathe our feasts and festivals.

For if there is no reconciliation,
    we cannot call Christ "Prince of Peace."
If there is no goodwill toward others,
    it can all be packed away in boxes for another year.
If there is no forgiveness in us,
    there is no cause for celebration.

If we cannot go now even unto Golgotha,
   there is no Christmas in us.
If Christmas is not *now*,
      If Christ is not born into the everyday present,
         then what is all the *noise* about?

STAR-GIVING

What I'd really like to give you for Christmas
Is a Star . . .
Brilliance in a package,
Something you could keep in the pocket of your jeans
Or in the pocket of your being,
Something to take out in times of darkness,
Something that would never snuff out or tarnish,
Something you could hold in your hand,
Something for wonderment,
Something for pondering,
Something that would remind you of
What Christmas has always meant:
God's Advent Light into the Darkness of this world.
But Stars are only God's for giving,
And I must be content to give you words and wishes and
Packages without Stars.
But I can wish you Life
As radiant as the Star
That announced the Christ Child's coming,
And as filled with awe as the Shepherds who stood
Beneath its Light,
And I can pass on to you the Love
That has been given to me,
Ignited countless times by others
Who have knelt in Bethlehem's Light.
Perhaps, if you ask, God will give you a Star.

O LORD, YOU WERE BORN!

Each year about this time I try to be sophisticated
And pretend I understand the bored expressions
                Relating to the "Christmas spirit."
I nod when they say "Put the Christ back in Christmas."
I say yes, yes, when they shout "Commercial" and
                "Hectic, hectic, hectic."
After all, I'm getting older,
And I've heard it said, "Christmas is for children."
But somehow a fa-la-la keeps creeping out . . .
So I'll say it:
I love Christmas tinsel
And angel voices that come from the beds upstairs.
And I say three cheers for Santa Claus
And the Salvation Army bucket
And all the wrappings and festivities and special warm feelings.
I say it is good
                Giving,
                Praising,
                Celebrating.
So hooray for Christmas trees
And candlelight
And the good old church pageant.
Hooray for shepherd boys who forget their lines
And wise men whose beards fall off
And a Mary who giggles.
O Lord, you were born!

O Lord, you were born!
And that breaks in upon my ordered life like bugles blaring,
And I sing "Hark, the Herald Angels" in the most unlikely places.
You were born
And I will celebrate!

I rejoice for the carnival of Christmas!
I clap for the pajama-clad cherubs
And the Christmas cards jammed in the mail slot.
I o-o-o-oh for the turkey
And ah-h-h-h for the Christmas pudding
And thank God for the alleluias I see in the faces of people
I don't know
        And yet know very well.

O Lord, there just aren't enough choir boys to sing what I feel.
There aren't enough trumpets to blow.
O Lord, I want bells to peal!
I want to dance in the streets of Bethlehem!
I want to sing with the heavenly host!
For unto us a Son was given
And he was called *God With Us.*
For those of us who believe,
The whole world is decorated in love!

LITANY OF HOPE
AND PROMISE

(This litany was written for the celebration of marriage for our son Stuart and his wife, Marina, but is appropriate for any two people entering into Christian marriage.)

Minister: O God, you are alive in all of life:

Be with us now as we gather to celebrate this new beginning.

People: Bless Stuart and Marina with fountains of goodness and love

As they enter into marriage, which was blessed by our Lord Jesus Christ.

Minister: As inheritors of the gift of Life, may their hearts be filled with thanksgiving for the abundance that is theirs because of your amazing grace.

People: May they take this inheritance and multiply it in a covenant relationship with you and with each other.

Minister: O God, we ask that their commitment be
undergirded by patience,
warmed by understanding,
enhanced by gratitude for each other.

People: May they look at each other and see;
May they listen to each other and hear;
May they speak to each other and encourage.

Minister: May they treasure all of Life as holy and precious.

People:	May their Life together be
	splashed with wonder,
	streaked with rainbows,
	touched by dreams.
Minister:	O God, who gave us spirits capable of love,
	Give to Stuart and Marina
	Faith that endures
	And hope that is pervasive;
People:	But above all else, let them be filled with the knowl-
	edge that
	Love never gives up.

WHERE IS THE CHURCH?

The church of Jesus Christ
    is where a child of God brings a balloon
    is where old women come to dance
    is where young men see visions and old men dream dreams

The church of Jesus Christ
    is where lepers come to be touched
    is where the blind see and the deaf hear
    is where the lame run and the dying live

The church of Jesus Christ
    is where daisies bloom out of barren land
    is where children lead and wise men follow
    is where mountains are moved and walls come tumbling
       down

The church of Jesus Christ
    is where loaves of bread are stacked in the sanctuary to feed
       the hungry
    is where coats are taken off and put on the backs of the naked
    is where shackles are discarded and kings and shepherds sit
       down in life together

The church of Jesus Christ
    is where barefoot children run giggling in procession
    is where the minister is ministered unto

is where the anthem is the laughter of the congregation and
    the offering plates are full of people

The church of Jesus Christ
    is where people go when they skin their knees or their hearts
    is where frogs become princes and Cinderella dances beyond
        midnight
    is where judges don't judge and each child of God is beautiful
        and precious

The church of Jesus Christ
    is where the sea divides for the exiles
    is where the ark floats and the lamb lies down with the lion
    is where people can disagree and hold hands at the same time

The church of Jesus Christ
    is where night is day
    is where trumpets and drums and tambourines declare God's
        goodness
    is where lost lambs are found

The church of Jesus Christ
    is where people write thank-you notes to God
    is where work is a holiday
    is where seeds are scattered and miracles are grown

The church of Jesus Christ
    is where home is
    is where heaven is
    is where a picnic is communion and people break bread
        together on their knees

The church of Jesus Christ
    is where we live responsively toward God's coming.
Even on Monday morning the world will hear
An abundance of alleluias!

THE CHURCH YEAR

(The following readings were used as part of a worship service at a regional meeting. We had a large wooden cross brought into the sanctuary and placed in the front. After each reading we draped the appropriate liturgical color on the cross. We used long pieces of gauze and arranged them so that each color could be seen.)

The church is Advent.
The unwrapping of God's greatest gift is near.
Advent—coming.
God will take away the tinsel
    and decorate our human hearts in hope
So that Christians can sit laughing in the rain,
    knowing that the Lord is going to
        shine in upon their being.
For no matter how long the darkness,
God will send the Light.
In spite of cursing and violence and the massacring of human
    dignity,
    we will dance in the streets of Bethlehem,
        for He will be born!

The church is Epiphany.
We are the Magi, searching,
Resplendent in this world's accouterments
    of knowledge and wealth and achievement.
But we search for something more

And—of all unlikely places—
    in a stable
        the Deity appears.
The borning of our Lord
    bursts in upon our ordinary lives
        like fireworks in the snow.
Only God would send a little baby King,
And we are on our knees,
Where we are within reach of our full personhood.

The church is Good Friday:
Blackness burnt into blackness,
Abysmal absence of anything good.
We acknowledge that death is real
And we tremble for a world that would kill its God.
Our feet stand in quicksand;
Our voices echo sterile silence.
We huddle together to meet the dark and the death,
Forgetting what was taught us,
Forgetting that somewhere
                a seed is sprouting,
        somewhere
                a child is growing.
All we see is Christ crucified.

The church is Easter.
Out of Death: Life.
Out of blackness: a lush green world,
            flowers in the ice,
            sunrays in the storm,
            mustard seeds galore.
Our souls enter a spiritual springtime,
Our bodies given over to leaping and dancing,
Our very beings saturated in hosannas.
Our shouting crashes in upon this world:
The Lord lives!
We live!
Resurrection resounds throughout our community.

The church is Pentecost.
The Holy Spirit is poured out upon us
And sends us out together
        aflame
            with new life,
Inheritors of the wealth of God:
                                Life abundant.
We are liberated from the prisons of pettiness,
        jealousy, and greed,
Liberated to be the church.

We are freed to free others.
We are affirmed to affirm others.
We are loved to love others.
We are family.
    We are community.
        We are the church triumphant—
You, me, anyone who would come unto the Lord—
Renewed, redirected, empowered
To change things and lives
Together in love and wholeness.
We are the Lord's church,
The church of justice and mercy,
The people sent to open prisons,
                to heal the sick,
                to clothe the naked,
                to feed the hungry,
                to reconcile,
To be alleluias when there is no music.
The mantle is upon our shoulders.
Joy is apparent in our living.
We have been commissioned to be the church of Jesus Christ.

SERVICES
OF
WORSHIP

GIFTS

(A service of thanksgiving and commitment, particularly appropriate during the Thanksgiving or Christmas season.)

CALL TO CELEBRATION

(Thanksgiving)
"The steadfast love of the Lord never ceases, mercies never come to an end; they are new every morning." (Lamentations 3:22–23)

(Christmas)
May we be innkeepers ready to find a place for our Lord,
May we be wise enough to follow a star.
May we be shepherds open to the possibility of miracles.
O Lord, may we find a kneeling place in that stable!
O come, O come, Emmanuel!
Enter here,
Enter now,
Find in us the angel's alleluia!

HYMN

(Thanksgiving): "Morning Has Broken"   Gaelic melody

(Christmas): "O Come, O Come, Emmanuel"
VENI EMMANUEL

85

Minister: Praise the name of God, who breathed life into our bodies.

People: Praise the name of God, who gave us a garden!

Minister: Praise the name of God, who saved us from the flood,

People: Who gave us a rainbow,

Minister: Who sent us the dove,

People: Who promised to be our God,

Minister: For we would be God's people.

People: Praise the name of God, who led us out of bondage,

Minister: Who parted the Red Sea and sent us manna,

People: Who sent the prophets,

Minister: Who called us from chaos to shalom.

People: Praise the name of God, who sent the Son.

Minister: All praise to God almighty!

People: Praise the name of God, who stills the waters,

Minister: Who gives us bread,

People: Who kills for us a fatted calf,

Minister: Who raises us from the dead;

People: Who never ceases looking for lost lambs,

Minister: Who saves us from self-righteousness,

People: Who heals our broken bodies,

Minister: Who calls us from our Sadducee and Pharisee religiosity,

People: Who challenges us to throw the first stone,

86

Minister:	Who gives us a cup of cold water
People:	And asks us to do the same for others,
Minister:	Who call us in Christ out of darkness into a new Light;
People:	Who gives us in Christ a new commandment:
Minister:	Love one another.
People:	Praise the name of God who weeps with us and laughs with us and calls us to believe.
Minister:	Praise the Lord God almighty!

ANTHEM

"Thank You, Thank You"   Avery and Marsh

READING OF THE SCRIPTURE   From Psalm 36

(This is beautiful as a choral reading, but it can also be read as follows:)

Reader 1:	Lord, your constant love reaches the heavens;
Reader 2:	Your faithfulness extends to the skies.
Reader 1:	Your righteousness is towering like the mountains;
Reader 2:	Your justice is like the depths of the sea.
Both:	People and animals are in your care.
Reader 1:	How precious, O God, is your constant love!
Reader 2:	We find protection under the shadow of your wings.
Reader 1:	We feast on the abundant food you provide.
Reader 2:	You let us drink from the river of your goodness.
Both:	You are the source of all life, and because of your light we see the light.

HYMN

(Thanksgiving): "We Gather Together to Ask the Lord's Blessing"   Netherlands folk song

(Christmas): "O Come, All Ye Faithful"   ADESTE FIDELES

THANK YOU FOR OTHERS

"Gift of God" (page 34)
"To You!" (page 31)

ROUND OF THANKS

"For all those others in our lives, we give you thanks, O Lord."

(This is the old camp round that you may have sung before meals: "For health and strength and daily food we praise thy name, O Lord." The choir director might take a few minutes to explain this round and how the congregation will sing it. The choir might start and then have the left side of the congregation come in, and then the right side. Each group sings the line three times.)

THANK YOU FOR GOD'S GIFTS

"Gifts from God" (page 65)

ANTHEM IN DANCE

"Day by Day," from *Godspell,* by Stephen Schwartz
or: "Mary Had a Baby"; Spiritual

(This is a lovely, quiet, modern dance with slow motions. It is worth the effort to find someone in your church or your community who is willing to try liturgical dance.)

OUR RESPONSE IN PRAISE AND THANKS

"Christmas Trees and Strawberry Summers" (page 29)

"Silver Spoons" (page 46)

AT THE OFFERING

(Choir director chooses a piece in keeping with the theme of thanksgiving and praise.)

OFFERTORY RESPONSE

"Praise God from Whom All Blessings Flow"

OLD HUNDREDTH

RESPONSE OF COMMITMENT

Minister: O God, you give us the morning sun and the evening star:

People: We have gathered to thank you.

Minister: O God, in you we live and move and have our being:

People: We have gathered to praise you.

Minister: O God, you bring us out of wilderness experiences into the Promised Land:

People: O God, we praise your name.

Minister: God of Grace,
Giver of Gifts,
Bless us we pray
As we seek to respond to your gift of Jesus Christ.

People: In Christ's name we thank you. Amen.

RECESSIONAL HYMN

"Praise to the Lord, the Almighty"   LOBE DEN HERREN

BENEDICTION

(Thanksgiving)
Thank you, God, for all that you have given and all that you
are giving. May we respond by giving to others. In the name
of Christ we pray. Amen.

(Christmas)
Go now into the world, carrying Christmas with you into
everyday life. Open the inn within you and make room for
that Gift of gifts, even our Lord Jesus Christ. Amen.

JESUS AND DANCING

For this service you will need a Messenger, a Chorus, a Teacher, a Pianist, a Soloist, a Dancer, and representative Voices. The Messenger will probably want to interact with the congregation, touching and moving among the people as he *or* she speaks. If possible, the room should be darkened as the service begins, except for a spotlight or even a large flashlight on the Messenger.

Messenger:

Are you a dancer who's never danced?
Are you a singer who's never sung?
Are you a laugher who holds it in?
Are you a weeper who's afraid to cry?
Are you someone who cares, but is afraid to risk love?
Do you have an alleluia deep inside you growing rusty?

In her book *Footnotes and Headlines,* Corita Kent quotes Jerome Murphy as saying: "If we left it to the Spirit there would be nothing in the church but Jesus and dancing." That's right. If we left it to the Spirit, there would be only the Way and the celebrating. The Love and the alleluias. The Living and the joy. The Gift and the thank you. The Song and the singing. The Good News and the shouting. But do we believe it? We're given abundance and we complain. Every day is a birthday and we walk around lifeless. God gives us Light and we close our eyes. God hands us Christmas and we yawn. The miracle is that God is always there, not dwelling on our chaos and our deadness, but offering us change:

Life—Joy—Song—Dance.

What would it take to snap you awake?

What would it take to make you alive and free to react, to respond, to live to God's music?

Once there was a time when you danced. Remember? You weren't afraid to dance then.

Once you could cry and laugh and dance and sing.

Once you could be angry and direct your anger appropriately. Once you could love fiercely.

"Unless you turn and become like children . . ."

When I think about Jesus and the children, I think about openness, about open arms—his and theirs.

I think about holding and cherishing.

I think about flowers and games in the sun.

I think about squealing and giggling and unrestrained laughter.

I think about the spirit with which he received them, accepting, loving, seeing the aliveness that adults often forfeit for security and prestige.

I think of their spirit, trusting, free, ready, eager.

"For of such is the kingdom."

Should we sh-h-h-h the Kingdom of God?

Chorus:

"Ring Around the Rosy"   Nursery rhyme

(Chorus sings softly and slowly while coming from the back of the sanctuary.)

Messenger:

Can you come as a little child?

Can you respond to God's music and care and dance and sing?

Hymn:

"Come as a Little Child"   Avery and Marsh

DANCE

> (*A Dancer with balloon, imitating a child, dances to the
> music of "Everything Is Beautiful."*)

*(At the end of the dance, the Teacher pops the Dancer's balloon.
The Chorus imitates a church school class, pushing, shoving,
laughing, giggling, and having a grand time until:)*

Teacher:

> Sh-h-h-h, sit down. Don't run in the church.
> Sh-h-h-h, sit down. Don't run in the church.
> Sh-h-h-h, sit down. Don't run in the church.

(Chorus settles down, and the Teacher speaks.)

Teacher:

> Now, children, what does Jesus tell us?

Chorus:

> Sh-h-h-h, sit down. Don't run in the church!

*(Chorus looks cowed and obedient. If possible have the Chorus
seated on straight chairs, sitting perfectly quietly.)*

(Lights out or dimmed.)

Messenger:

> *(spotlighted)* And what do we want to tell the children?

Chorus:

> Jesus Christ says, comb your hair.

Messenger:

> And what do we want to tell the children?

Chorus:

> Jesus Christ says, sit on your chair.

Messenger:

> And what do we want to tell the children?

Chorus:

> Jesus Christ says, be polite.

Messenger:
> And what do we want to tell the children?

Chorus:
> Jesus says, do everything right!
> Jesus says, please sit down.
> Jesus says, do not frown.
> Jesus says, don't cry if you're hurt.
> Jesus says, don't play in the dirt.
> Jesus says, do not run.
> Jesus says, don't have any fun!

Messenger:
> And what do we want to tell the children?

Chorus:
> We want to tell them sh-h-h-h.

(Lights out briefly. When lights come back up, the Chorus is either lying on the floor asleep or sitting in chairs asleep.)

Messenger:
> But you're not children anymore.
> This is the church grown up. Wake up!
> Isn't this the church of Jesus Christ?

(Chorus stretches and yawns and gets up and joins arms.)

Messenger:
> Isn't this the church?

(Chorus nods yes.)

Messenger:
> Well, may I come in?

Chorus:
> *(looking over Messenger, scrutinizing)* He (she) looks like
> us. He (she) talks like us. Okay, come in.

(All sit down in a group.)

Chorus:
> And so, we want to do all that's right and all that's good.
> *(Said rather preachily and piously.)*

Messenger:
> A-A-men! A-A-men! A-A-A-A-A-men!

(Messenger sings and snaps fingers. Chorus stares at Messenger, who stops singing.)

Chorus:
> Now we'll have the closing hymn.

(Choose a familiar tune. Messenger begins to dance and clap hands as the music starts. Chorus stares again and then locks arms, shutting the Messenger out. Pianist plays a discordant note and the lights go out. Spotlight is then on the Messenger.)

Messenger:
> We believe in Jesus Christ—the Way, the Truth, the Life.
> There's something discordant in the words and the living.
> We say dance, but we crawl.
> We say peace, but we gather arms.
> We say Life, but we kill.
> We say joy, but we repress.
> We say hope, but we give up.
> We say community, but we divide.
> We say celebrate, but we yawn.
> We say give, but we take.
> We say good news, but we mean ho-hum.
> We say we are our brother's and our sister's keeper, but we
>   don't do anything about it.
> We moralize about people who are hungry.
> We shake our fingers at kids who are drugged.
> We gossip about those who threaten us.
> We ridicule those who are different.
> We ignore the needs of the elderly
> We turn our backs to the lonely.
> We condone morals that violate personhood:

a little lying,
a little cheating,
a little obscenity won't hurt.
We say law and order, but we mean law and order for
them.
We say where your heart is there is your treasure also—
And if it's true, our treasures turn out to be:
a clean kitchen floor,
a skinny figure,
a move to the right neighborhood.
Our gods are football players, politicians, and rock singers.
Our altar is the TV set or a sports car or a neatly manicured
lawn.
And we sing loud praises
to the newest deodorant,
to redoing the kitchen,
to anything that makes us look younger.
All praise to things and correctness.

Chorus:
We believe in Jesus Christ:
All praise to things and correctness.
We believe in Jesus Christ:
All praise to things and correctness.
We believe in closed doors and closed lives.
Who do you say that he is?
We believe in complaining and pettiness.
Who do you say that he is?
We believe in wringing our hands.
Who do you say that he is?
We believe in tabling the controversial.
Who do you say that he is?
We believe in "my church is better than your church."
Who do you say that he is
By the way you live?

(Pianist plays another discordant note on the piano. Then suddenly Chorus with toy machine guns, helmets, and noisemakers runs

*up and down the aisles, pushing, shoving, poking at people.
All the while discordant music is playing. Chorus brings people who have previously agreed to be taken to the front of the
church. There the people are "crucified." Lights out or
dimmed.)*

Messenger:

I'd like to see a little outrage please.
That's part of knowing Christ's dance.
Dance into the temple and push a few tables over.
I'd like to see a little outrage please.
I'd like to hear some voice rise out of the chaos.
I'd like to hear a little righteous indignation.
Christ's church is mired down in divisiveness and nobody's
    angry?
A child's balloon is popped and nobody cares?
Is it all right with you that people are shouting obscenities
    at each other in Christ's name?
Is it all right that churches are splitting down the middle
    in Christ's name?
Is it all right with you that children in church school are
    being taught an irrelevant Jesus?
Is it all right with you that Christians sit in their pews
    lifeless?
Could I hear a little weeping please for
    the children that nobody claims,
    the elderly that nobody claims,
    the hungry that nobody claims,
    the alcoholics that nobody claims,
    the diseased that nobody claims,
    the hurt that nobody claims,
    the displaced that nobody claims,
    the poverty-riddled that nobody claims.
Could I hear a little outrage please?
Is it all right with you that someone who looks different or
    talks different or acts different is not welcome in the
    church of Jesus Christ?
Aren't you outraged that we even have to discuss it?

They're pulling people right out of the pews and no one's
   objected!
O children of Israel, why don't you gnash your teeth?
Why don't you wail?
Your people are dying!

(Lights out or dimmed. Out of the darkness a voice speaks.)

Voice:

Sh-h-h-h, sit down. Don't run in the church. She looks like
   us. She comes from a good family. Come in. Come
   in. War. Blood. Violence. Cheat. Hate. Hurt. Gossip.
   Bruise. Things. More. Money. More money. Mine.
   Kill. My God is a clean kitchen floor. I'm too busy,
   kid. Sh-h-h-h. Ignore. My church is better than your
   church. Exploit sex. Rob. Shove. Rape. Kick. Obscenities. Things. You are a thing. You are a thing.
   You are a thing. *Chaos!* Help-p-p-p. . . .

*(Lights begin to come on, but are still low. Pianist and Chorus lead
   the congregation in singing.)*

Hymn:

"O Lamb of God"   *Agnus Dei*

Messenger:

(spotlighted) Who can say Hope in the midst of Chaos
   when every answer is death?

Voice:

The people that walked in darkness have seen a great light;
   they that dwell in the land of the shadow of death,
   upon them hath the light shined. . . . For unto us a
   child is born, unto us a son is given; and the government shall be upon his shoulder; and his name shall
   be called Wonderful, Counselor, The mighty God,
   The everlasting Father, The Prince of Peace.
Walk as children of light—for the fruit of the Spirit is in
   all goodness and righteousness and truth. Awake thou
   that sleepest, and arise from the dead, and Christ
   shall give thee light. . . . Be filled with the Spirit;

speaking to yourselves in psalms and hymns and spiritual songs, singing and making melody in your heart to the Lord.

Praise the Lord's name in the dance: Let them sing praises unto the Lord with the timbrel and harp. . . . Praise the Lord! (From Isaiah 9:2, 6; Ephesians 5:8–9, 14, 19; Psalm 149:3)

Solo:

"Over My Head I Hear Music"   Spiritual

HYMN:

"I Danced in the Morning"

Words and arrangement by Sydney Carter

(Dancer dances to "I Danced in the Morning" *while congregation sings.)*

Messenger:

Is there an alleluia deep inside you growing rusty?
Awake and stand in the light.
Praise God's name with singing and dancing!
Unbutton yourselves and stand open to catch the wind.
May they say of us: They are drunk on new wine . . . the new wine of the Spirit!

(Messenger and Chorus recess out, following Dancer, as the Pianist plays another verse of "I Danced in the Morning.")

Messenger:

There is no end to this service; the Lord's dance goes on forever!

(Pianist plays "I Danced in the Morning" *as the people dance out.)*

A GROUP OF BELIEVERS
A Service of Worship for Pentecost

(The service begins with a celebrant reading the call to worship from the back of the sanctuary prior to the processional. Choir and participants join in the processional.)

CALL TO WORSHIP: Acts 2:1–2

PROCESSIONAL: "The Day of Pentecost Arrived"
Frank A. Brooks, Jr.

RESPONSE

Celebrant 1:
>The service today is centered on the Pentecost Scripture found in the second chapter of Acts. *(Pause.)*
>The believers are gathered together in one place, And they hear the noise of a world screaming:

Celebrant 2:
>The swelling, anguished cries of the outcasts;
>The piercing pleas of the battle-scarred, innocent or not—their lives disrupted and maimed and smashed;

Celebrant 3:
>The devastating death rattle of those who hungered and were not fed;
>The outraged voice of the oppressed who don't even see the faces of the people walking on them;

Celebrant 4:

The unrelenting beating of fists against the walls of prejudice and apathy and greed;

The fearful cry of the abandoned wafting out into a world that doesn't even bother to turn and see who's crying;

Celebrant 5:

The sobs of the lonely, the untouched—the round pegs who simply do not fit into the world's preconceived squares,

The tired moaning of those who have given up,

Celebrant 2:

And the litany of the chained:

All: (Both

Let me free! Let me free!

Celebrant 1:

The believers are gathered in one place. Where two or three are gathered together in Christ's name . . .

Celebrant 2:

But do the believers know Christ's name?
Christ's name is not Tradition.

Celebrant 3: /

Christ's name is Newness.

Celebrant 2:

Christ's name is not Oppression.

Celebrant 3: /

It is Justice.

Celebrant 2:

Christ's name is not Self-Righteousness.

Celebrant 3: /

It is Humility.

Celebrant 2:

Christ's name is not Chastisement.

Celebrant 3:
It is Mercy.

Celebrant 2:
Christ's name is not Aloneness.

Celebrant 3:
It is Community.

Celebrant 2:
Christ's name is not Ordinariness.

Celebrant 3:
It is Life—
Abundant, plentiful, multiflavored Life!

Celebrant 4:
Christ's name is Risk.
Christ's name is Giving.
Christ's name is Healing.
Christ's name is Accepting.

Celebrant 5:
Christ's name is Tear-the-Walls-Down.
Christ's name is Out-in-the-Marketplace.
Christ's name is Walk-the-Streets-and-Find-My-Hurting-People.
Christ's name is Feed-My-Sheep.

Celebrant 4:
Christ's name is Changed Lives.
Christ's name is New Creation.
Christ's name is Love Them.

Celebrant 5:
Christ's name is Love.

Celebrant 1:
Where one or two are gathered together in Love there
Christ is also. The strong wind blows and it fills the
whole house—Christ's church—and nothing is ordinary anymore.

HYMN: "Come, Holy Ghost, Our Souls Inspire"

VENI CREATOR SPIRITUS

SCRIPTURE: Acts 2:3–4

Call to worship ⌐

LITANY OF HOPE

Celebrants: *One*

The believers speak in different tongues,

People: *All*

For they have been given different gifts.

Celebrants:

We are gathered here today that our lives may be touched
by tongues of fire.

People:

We are gathered here today that our hearts may become
flames of warmth to a cold world.

Celebrants:

We are gathered today to be open to the possibility of your
Holy Spirit.

People:

Fill us, Lord.

Celebrants:

Come down upon us, Descending Dove,

People:

And enable us to speak the Truth to your world. *Amen!*

All:

Amen. ⌐

SCRIPTURE: Acts 2:5–7

CONFESSION OF FAITH

Prayer

O God, we confess our amazement and confusion in the face of ⌐

your truth. Our eyes have not been looking for your tongues of fire. Our hearts have not been open to be filled. Our gifts have gone unused, and we have not appreciated the gifts of others. Descend upon us, Holy Spirit, that our lives may reflect your glory. In the name of Jesus Christ, in whose name we pray. Amen.

SCRIPTURE: Acts 2:22–24, 41–47

HYMN: "The Lone, Wild Bird"   McFadyen; PROSPECT

(As the congregation is settling down after the hymn, go directly into the following play. You will need several people. A good number of them will be church members who will do some singing and some moving, but will not have any speaking parts. The play begins with two people sitting on either side of the sanctuary. Change the denomination name to your own.)

Leader 1:   Once upon a now, there were in the same town two Presbyterian churches. No one thought that particularly strange. After all, there had always been two Presbyterian churches.

Leader 2:   First Presbyterian Church, Main Street, and Second Presbyterian Church, Main Street.

(Two groups of people enter from either side. They carry signs identifying themselves as First or Second Church members.)

Leader 1:   And there was a good-hearted competition between the two churches.

Leader 2:   Led by their two good-hearted ministers.

First Minister: *(in singsong voice)* My church is better than your church.

Second Minister:	*(in singsong voice)* Anything you can do, we can do better.
First:	I'm proud of our church!
Second:	We have more members.
First:	Ten percent of our members are Ph.D.'s!
Second:	We have a better choir.
First:	We give more to the poor.
Second:	We have a bigger building.
First:	We have an innovative church school.
Second:	We have to have three services to get everybody in!
First:	We have guitars at worship.
Second:	Well, I've been known to give rather superior sermons.
First:	I ride a motorcycle to go calling. Besides, I've been nominated to go to the national assembly next spring.
Second:	I went last year.
First:	We do more for this community.
Second:	We have more overseas mission projects.
First:	We have more discussion groups.
Second:	We have more prayer groups.
First:	*(pausing, trying to think)* We have dance in worship!
Second:	*(gleefully)* Well, we don't!

(People from each church sing:)

Left Side:	Our church is better than your church.

Right Side:	Anything you can do, we can do better.
Left Side:	No, you can't.
Right Side:	Yes, we can.

(This continues until stopped by Leader 1, who raises his or her hand to silence them.)

Leader 1:	One day a little child who didn't know any better wandered from one church to the other.

(The child, wearing a sign that reads CHILD OF GOD, carries a balloon or a lollipop. The child goes from First Church to Second Church.)

Child:	I'm a little child who doesn't know any better.

(Child knocks on "door" of Second Church.)

Gruff:	Who are you?
Child:	I'm a child of God.
Gruff:	Yeah? Well, you don't belong here!
Child:	*(stamping feet)* Well, I want in!

(If possible, put a spotlight on the Reader—representing the voice of conscience—and dim all other lights. If you have no spot, have all the other people in the play turn their backs to the congregation while the Reader speaks.)

Reader:	What do we want to tell the children?
	Jesus Christ says, comb your hair.
	And what do we want to tell the children?
	Jesus Christ says, sit on your chair.
	And what do we want to tell the children?
	Jesus Christ says, be polite.
	And what do we want to tell the children?
	Jesus says, do everything right!
	Jesus says, please sit down.
	Jesus says, do not frown.

Jesus says, don't cry if you're hurt.
Jesus says, don't play in the dirt.
Jesus says, do not run.
Jesus says, don't have any fun!
And what do we want to tell the children?
We want to tell them sh-h-h-h.

Chorus: *(The Chorus is composed of everybody else in the play)*
Sh-h-h-h, sit down; don't run in the church!
Sh-h-h-h, sit down; don't run in the church!
Sh-h-h-h, sit down; don't run in the church!
Sh-h-h-h-h-h!

(Lights back up, or people in play turn around.)

Leader 2: Now there was in this church an old woman who was thought by some to be a little senile.

(Old Woman appears with identifying sign: OLD WOMAN.*)*

Old Woman: Who's that at the door?

Gruff: Says he (she) is a child of God. I explained that he (she) was in the wrong place.

Child: I want in!

Old Woman: Come in, come in.

(Old Woman sings solo the first verse of "Come as a Little Child," by Avery and Marsh. For the second verse, she motions to the congregation to rise and join her. The words should, of course, be available to them.)

Child: Would you please pray for my friend, Tim? His daddy got arrested for embezzlement and he didn't even do it. My mother says you've got lots of prayer groups at this church!

107

Gruff: We shouldn't get involved in this sort of thing!

(Light on Reader, or backs of the remaining participants turned, as directed previously.)

Reader: O church, where are you?
Children of God knock upon your door
And you do not recognize them.
They cry to you for mercy
And you don't want to get involved.
They come to you for help
And you close the door in their faces.
O church, where are you in the midst of
Tears and hunger and pain?
Where are you when darkness
Envelops my people?
O church, call my people to you
And hold them in the Light!

(Lights back up or people turn around to face the congregation.)

Old Woman: Of course, we'll pray for Tim and his daddy.

(Group from Second Church kneel one by one as they sing softly "Day by Day," from Godspell, *by Stephen Schwartz.)*

Old Woman: *(to Child)* I hear you have dancing in your church.

Child: Yes, we do.

Old Woman: I don't suppose—uh—do you think—could you take me to see? I've always wanted to dance.

Child: *(taking her hand)* Sure.

Leader 1:   Hand in hand, the child who didn't know any better and the old woman who wanted to dance went to the other church, First Church.

(Scolding, a member of First Church who also wears an identifying sign steps out from the group toward Child of God and Old Woman.)

Scolding: Child of God! Where have you been? Didn't you know we'd be worried about you?

Child: I went to find somebody to pray. This is my friend. She wants to be a dancer.

Scolding: This is the dancer?

(Old Woman raises hands above her head and snaps her fingers in response.)

Scolding: *(addressing the congregation)* This looks like that Old Woman who is thought by some to be a little senile.

(Light on Reader or backs turned.)

Reader: Are there no dances for gray-haired children
                   Whose hearts still tap to the sound of joy?
                   Are there no steps for feet that falter
                   But whose music still beats as it did before?
                   Is there no dancing for God's still faithful
                        whose spirits shout,
                             whose love overflows?
                   Are there no dances for gray-haired children?

(Young Woman with identifying sign steps out of First Church.)

Young Woman: Who's there?

Scolding: Oh, it's just Child of God with some old woman who thinks she's a dancer.

Young Woman: Come in, come in. Any friend of Child of God's is a friend of mine

Child: She wants to dance.

Young Woman: Why not?

(They join hands and others from First Church dance with them.)

HYMN: "Pass It On"   Ralph Carmichael; Kurt Kaiser

(Everyone, congregation included, sings the hymn while the group from First Church "dances." Perhaps some could dance down into the congregation, or special dancers might dance down the aisle and touch members of the congregation as they pass by. When hymn and dancing are finished, Young Woman steps out and speaks.)

Young Woman: Don't you have an excellent choir at your church? I'd love to sing with them.

Old Woman: *(taking Young Woman and Child of God by their hands and starting toward Second Church)*
Well, come on, then!

HYMN

(Choose a hymn familiar to your congregation and have the congregation join in on the second verse. When the hymn is finished, Old Man steps forward from Second Church.)

Old Man: I wonder if your church would like some good used clothing for the thrift shop you run. In our church we give money, but we have no program for giving clothing.

Young Woman: We sure could use it!

(They all walk to First Church.)

Another Woman: *(member of First Church)* I've been wanting to hear your minister preach. I don't suppose . . .

(All hurriedly leave.)

Young Man: *(stepping out from Second Church group)*
Why don't we all work on that project

that you at First Church have started—
the one where you help downtown tenants fix up their houses?

(They all walk to First Church . . . then back to Second . . . back and forth. Pianist plays music that gets faster and faster until it is running music. Then when the music stops abruptly all freeze in place.)

Leader 2:   The two churches began to pray together, to dance together, to feed the hungry together, to give to the poor, to do justice, to love mercy, to walk humbly with God. Before they knew it, they weren't sure who had been members of First Church and who had been members of Second Church. They just knew they were members of the Church of Jesus Christ. What had happened was this: They had heard a noise like a rushing wind and they had been touched by tongues of fire. They were filled with the Spirit of Love, which is only given by God. No longer were they busy with listening to pettiness and no longer did their eyes see only the fault in others. Now in their common mission they thanked God for each other.

(Light on Reader, or backs turned to direct attention to Reader.)

Reader: "Gift of God" (page 34)

HYMN: "There Is a Balm in Gilead"   Spiritual

PRAYER: O God, we would be the church of Jesus Christ, together and in Christ's name. Amen.

The Passing of the Peace

(Each person is asked to turn to those nearby and, with words of affirmation and hope, to greet them.)

RECESSIONAL: "We Are One in the Spirit"   Peter Scholtes

LIFE ABUNDANT

WELCOME

The worship service today concerns the church and lepers and the good news. It's about the Christian's responsibility to share the sunshine with the "untouchables"—the poor, the captives, the blind, the oppressed. It's about wholeness and life abundant, for that's what Christ said he came for. Join us!

CALL TO WORSHIP IN SONG: "Sing Love Songs"

Avery and Marsh

(The choir from the back of the sanctuary will sing the first two stanzas. The congregation will join in as the choir and the participants process down the aisle.)

CHANCEL DRAMA: "THE CHURCH AND LEPERS"

(The participants, representing the Church and Scripture, process down the aisle with the Choir on the third stanza of the preceding hymn. Church Members 1, 2, 3, 4, and 5 sit on stools in the chancel. Scripture Readers 1 and 2 stand on either side in lectern and pulpit.)

Scripture Reader 1:   "The Spirit of the Lord is upon me,
because he has chosen me to preach the
Good News to the poor.
He has sent me to proclaim liberty to
the captives,

and recovery of sight to the blind;
to set free the oppressed,
and announce the year when the Lord
will save his people." (Luke 4:16–19,
TEV)

Member 5:	They're out there again.
Member 1:	Oh, for heaven's sake, you're always hearing things. Let's get on with the meeting. We've got decisions to make. I for one think we ought to redecorate.
Member 2:	Redecorate?
Member 1:	Everything. The sanctuary . . . the church school . . . the whole building.
Member 4:	It won't work.
Member 2:	What about our priorities? Is that what the church is all about? Redecorating? What about Bible study? What about prayer?
Member 1:	We can have Bible study and prayer in the newly decorated building.
Member 4:	We've never done it that way before.
Member 3:	I don't think we should put money into decorating. We've got to get going with this tutoring program. Social action is the answer.
Member 4:	It won't work.
Member 5:	Don't you hear anything?
Member 1:	There's nobody there, I tell you!
Member 5:	Don't any of you hear them?
Member 2:	It's just the wind. Look, why don't we start a prayer group?

Member 4:	It won't work.
Member 2:	Why?
Member 4:	We've never done it that way before.
Member 5:	They're crying. . . .
Member 3:	Look, the rest of us are here to make decisions, to discover priorities for the life of the church. We don't hear anything. This is an important meeting tonight. We're here to decide where we as Christians should put all our efforts, our money, our time, our energy. That's why I say we need action. I propose we join that group of protesters on Sunday.
Member 1:	Oh, no, not this Sunday. I think we ought to have a paint party Sunday afternoon. After all, we're supposed to get the mote out of our own eye first, you know! Everybody could come for the day. After church we could eat our sandwiches and we could have coffee and dessert and . . .
Member 2:	On Sunday? At least on Sunday let's use the church for worship!
Member 3:	Well, people worship in different ways. I can't think of a more worshipful way to spend a Sunday than protesting!
Member 2:	Praying!
Member 1:	Painting!
Member 4:	It won't work!
Member 5:	Surely you hear them now. They're calling us!

Members 1, 2, 3, 4:   Who?

Member 5:   The lepers of this world.

(Lepers start down the aisle from the back of the sanctuary. They are wailing "Help!" "Peace!" "Justice!" "Love!")

Member 5:   They need us.

(Member 5 starts down the steps toward the lepers, and the others hold 5 back.)

Member 3:   Do you want to get infected?

Member 1:   Let's lock the doors!

Scripture Reader 1:   "You lock the door to the Kingdom of heaven in people's faces, but you yourselves will not go in, and neither will you let people in who are trying to go in!" (Matt. 23:13, TEV alt.)

(Lepers reach steps.)

Leper: A leper am I and no one will touch me
For fear they'll be contaminated.
I have been cast outside the church,
Locked out of Christ's church,
Shunned and cast away from society,
Covered with sores of my differentness,
Outcast because of my poverty and hunger,
Because of my race, my sex, my skin's color,
Because of my clothes, my manners, my environment,
Because of my youth, my politics, my old age,
Because of my mental illness, my divorce, my nationality.
Because of my beard, my dialect, my family background, my job . . .

I am in pain—the pain of prejudice.

I am imprisoned by the deeds and words of others.

I am fragmented and sick and long for wholeness.

I am covered with the boils of loneliness, fear, and depression.

I am oppressed . . . stained and spit upon and beaten

And given only a small corner in which to do my bleeding.

O Church, give me justice!

O Church, give me mercy!

O Church, give me love.

Christians, touch me, heal me,

Share your sanctuary.

Give me life abundant.

Let me live in the sunshine!

All Lepers: You can heal us if you want to!

(Members 1, 2, 3, and 4 turn around one by one, until their backs are to the congregation.)

Choir: First verse of "Sing Love Songs" Avery and Marsh

Member 5: I'll get help for you! *(Goes to Member 1)*
Hey, the world is calling for us.
It's broken and it's limping and it's blind.

The world is calling for us
And it's time we found the time.

Member 1: I'm sorry, but I'm busy with this redecorating.

Member 5: *(to 2)* Hey, the world is calling to us.
It's hungry and it's cold and it's sighing.
The world is calling for us
And it's time we found the time.

117

Member 2:	Sorry, I've got a prayer meeting.
Member 5:	*(to 3)* Hey, the world is calling for us. It's sick and it's lonely and it's crying. The world is calling for us And it's time we found the time.
Member 3:	Sorry, but I've got a meeting for peace and justice.
Member 5:	*(to 4)* Hey, the world is calling for us. It's oppressed and it's orphaned and it's dying. The world is calling for us And it's time we gave the time.
Member 4:	Sorry, but it won't work. Besides, we've never done it that way before.
Scripture Reader 2:	He said, "I am come that they might have life, and that they might have it more abundantly." (John 10:10, KJV)
Member 5:	Hey, church, the world is calling for us. The people are crying for us. O God, save the people!

HYMN: "Save the People"

From *Godspell,* by Stephen Schwartz

(During the singing the lepers parade with signs: LOVE FOR LEP-ERS; I WANT TO BE TOUCHED; I WANT TO LIVE IN THE SUNSHINE; SHARE YOUR SANCTUARY.*)*

Member 5:	*(sitting on the steps)* It's no wonder the parade's out there. It's dark in here. It's cold. It's lifeless. It's no wonder the parade's out there, Where the sun is, Where the music is,

Where the daisies grow.
It's no wonder the parade's out there,
Where the birds sing,
Where the dreams are,
Where the children play.
It's no wonder . . .
How can you have a parade in silence?
How can you have a peopleless, musicless
    parade?
It's no wonder the parade's out there.
O God, save your people!
O God, bring the parade into your church!

Leper Dancer: If you want to, you can make me clean.

Member 5:   I do want to help you.

Scripture Reader 1:   "This is my commandment, that you love one another as I have loved you." (John 15:12)

(Leper and Member 5 kneel together and 5 reaches out slowly and touches Leper. Leper stands slowly and begins to dance to "Day by Day" from Godspell, *by Stephen Schwartz, while the Choir sings the words. Dance ends with Leper and Member 5 knocking on the church door. There Members 1, 2, 3, and 4 "stone" them. They fall.)*

Scripture Reader 2:   "How terrible for you, teachers of the Law and Pharisees! Hypocrites! You lock the door to the Kingdom of heaven in people's faces, but you yourselves will not go in, and neither will you let people in who are trying to go in.

Scripture Reader 1:   "How terrible for you . . . You take advantage of widows and rob them of their homes, and then make a show of saying long prayers! Because of this your punishment will be all the worse!

Scripture Reader 2: "How terrible for you! You give to God one tenth even of the seasoning herbs, such as mint, dill, and cummin, but you neglect to obey the really important teachings of the Law, such as justice and mercy and honesty. . . . Blind guides! You strain a fly out of your drink, but swallow a camel!

Scripture Reader 1: "You clean the outside of your cup and plate, while the inside is full of things you have gotten by violence and selfishness.

Scripture Reader 2: "You are like whitewashed tombs, which look fine on the outside, but are full of dead men's bones and rotten stuff on the inside. In the same way, on the outside you appear to everybody as good, but inside you are full of hypocrisy and sins.

Scripture Reader 1: "Jerusalem, Jerusalem! You kill the prophets and stone the messengers God has sent you! How many times have I wanted to put my arms around all your people, just as a hen gathers her chicks under her wings, but you would not let me! Now your home will be completely forsaken. From now on you will never see me again, I tell you, until you say, 'God bless him who comes in the name of the Lord.' " (From Matthew 23:13–39, TEV)

LITANY OF CONFESSION

(Members 1, 2, 3, 4, and 5 are the Church. The response is made by the congregation.)

Church:	O God, your people were upon our door-step, beaten and stepped upon,
People:	And we did not see them.
Church:	You screamed their agony into our ears,
People:	And we did not hear them.
Church:	Your people bled upon us,
People:	And all we could think about was removing the stains.
Church:	Your people cried to us for sanctuary,
People:	And we locked the church door.
Church:	O God, we seek to comfort
People:	Ourselves;
Church:	O God, we seek to help
People:	Ourselves;
Church:	We seek to trust
People:	Ourselves;
All:	God, forgive us.
Church:	O God, your people were abused and chained and passed over. Your people were shoved and demeaned and ridiculed.
People:	And we could not risk seeing or hearing.
Church:	O God, your people were treated as lepers,
People:	And we could not risk touching them.
Church:	Give us the justice
People:	That we could not give others.

Church:	Give us the mercy
People:	That we would not give others.
Church:	Give us the closeness to you
People:	That we tried to keep from others.
Church:	Give us the Good News
People:	That we hoarded.
All:	O God, save your people—both outcasts and church!

ANTHEM: "Sanctus," from the *Rejoice Mass*

(During the singing, Members 1, 2, 3, and 4 go to the lepers and remove their hoods. They put their arms around them as Member 5 reads.)

Member 5:   Bring the parade in here.
Bring the sunshine and the music and the flowers.
Bring the drums in here.
Bring the singing, bring the clapping, bring the children.

Bring the parade in here.
Bring the hurting and the healing and the dreaming.
Break the silence in here.
Bring the trumpets and the colors and the cheering.

Bring the love in here.
Bring the world in here.
Bring the sunshine into the sanctuary.
Bring the parade in here!

Scripture Reader 1:   God's people will shine like the sun.

Recessional: "He's Got the Whole World in His Hands"
Spiritual

Benediction
Go now to parade Good News throughout God's world.

CELEBRATE THE CHILDREN

PRELUDE

MEDITATION: "Listen to Our Children"

(Play back the taped voices of church school children answering questions such as: How do you know Jesus loves you? Who is God? Why do your parents come to church? Why do they want you to come to church? What is your favorite thing about church? Note: When we asked these questions, the answers were everything we had hoped for!)

CALL TO WORSHIP

> Let us worship the Lord, who came not as a king but as a babe. Let us worship the Lord, who said: "Let the little children come unto me, and forbid them not; for of such is the kingdom of God." (Mark 10:14)

WELCOME

(Welcome the worshipers in the usual way, and then add:)

> This morning we are celebrating the children. "Jesus called a child, had him stand in front of them, and said . . . 'The greatest in the Kingdom of heaven is the one who humbles himself and becomes like this child. And whoever welcomes in my name one such child as this, welcomes me.'" (Matthew 18:2–5, TEV.) In

the name of Jesus we welcome each of you this morning, each child of God. "For of such is the Kingdom." Should we sh-h-h-h the Kingdom of God or should we pass out lollipops?

We have a banner here in the front of the sanctuary. It is centered with two embracing figures, that of an adult and that of a child. The banner symbolizes children's needs and the world's response. Our children have made symbols that express their thoughts and feelings about church. We ask that the children come forward now and place their symbols on the banner.

(The symbols should be made several weeks prior to the service during the church school hour. Children who are absent that Sunday should have a later opportunity to make a symbol. Prepare extra symbols for those who might be attending for the first time today.)

PROCESSION OF CHILDREN AND HYMN: "Come as a Little Child"
Avery and Marsh

(As the children place their symbols on the banner, the choir will sing the first verse of "Come as a Little Child." The congregation will then join the choir in singing. Members of the worship committee should sit on the first row and come up and help the children should they need any help pinning their symbols onto the banner. Later the symbols can be glued on and the banner can be hung where everyone can see it.)

MEDITATION: "What Do We Want to Tell the Children?"

Sometimes in the rush and crunch of our mission as God's children, we forget who we are: the children of God. In our grown-up practicality, in our busy-busy adult-conscience productivity, we forget that Christ said, "Unless you become as little children, you shall not enter into the kingdom of heaven." We even forget who he is, and we begin telling the story all wrong.

LITANY OF CONFESSION: "The Lord of Life" (page 26)

(Read responsively, Minister and People, beginning with the line "O Jesus, you were real" and ending with the line "O Lord! We paid no attention to who you are: the Lord of Life!" Add the following response of the people:)

People: This morning we would come as children—
        Humble, innocent, spontaneous, and trusting.
        We come, your children, ready to hear
        The possibility of your Word. Amen.

ANTHEM: "Jacob and Sons"   Webber and Rice
    From *Joseph and the Amazing Technicolor Dreamcoat*

THE SACRAMENT OF BAPTISM

HYMN OF RESPONSE *(Congregation):* "Jesus Loves Me"

READING: "ALL THE CHILDREN OF THE WORLD"

Minister: What about the children of this world who are not filled with life's joys? What about the children who are have-nots—who have not food, have not clothing and medicine, have not warm shelter, and have not parents? What about the abused or neglected child? What about the child who lives in darkness?

First Reader: Gabriela Mistral, Nobel prize-winning poet from Chile, has written: "We are guilty of many errors and many faults, but our worst crime is abandoning the children, neglecting the fountain of life. Many of the things we need can wait. The child cannot. Right now is the time his bones are being formed, his blood is being made, and his senses are being developed. To

126

him we cannot answer 'Tomorrow.' His name is 'Today.' "

Second Reader: Luchi Blanco from Cuzco, Peru, has said: "Nor clothes, nor language, nor color, nor nation can change the soul of the child; in kissing, in crying, and in song the children of the world are one."

Third Reader: These words were spoken when UNICEF (the United Nations Children's Fund) received the Nobel Prize for Peace in 1965: "Feeling is growing everywhere . . . that we are in reality one family in the world . . . to create a peaceful world, we must begin with the children."

Minister: The United Nations has declared that every child in this world should have certain rights:

"The right to affection, love and understanding.

The right to adequate nutrition and medical care.

The right to free education.

The right to full opportunity for play and recreation.

The right to a name and nationality.

The right to special care, if handicapped.

The right to be among the first to receive relief in times of disaster.

The right to be a useful member of society and to develop individual abilities.

The right to be brought up in a spirit of peace and universal brotherhood.

The right to enjoy these rights, regardless of race, color, sex, religion, national or social origin."

PRAYER

God of all nations, God of all children, we ask for your mercy on behalf of all the children who do not run in the sunshine but live out their lives in dark corners. Forgive

127

us for not seeing; forgive us for not looking. Be with us as we search for new beginnings in caring for these children. We pray that one day every child might sleep through the night in peace.

CHORAL RESPONSE: "Sleep, My Child, and Peace Attend Thee All Through the Night"   Welsh melody

CHILDREN'S SONGS

(This is a very special time for the children to share their favorite songs.)

OLD TESTAMENT LESSON

(Fourth Reader):

The people who walked in darkness have seen a great light ... for unto us a child is born, to us a son is given; and the government will be upon his shoulder, and his name will be called "Wonderful Counselor, Mighty God, Everlasting Father, Prince of Peace." (From Isaiah 9:2, 6)

NEW TESTAMENT LESSON

(First Reader):

Jesus said, "Let the little children come unto me, and forbid them not; for of such is the kingdom of God." (Mark 10:14)

READING

(Second Reader):

"Greenless Child" (page 33)

READING

(All four Readers):

"A Group of Believers"

(Read as divided on page 44, adding a last line for Fourth Reader:
It is written: "A little child shall lead them.")

DIALOGUE:
"What Do You Think About Church, Michael?"

(This is an informal dialogue between a parent and child concerning the child's thoughts and feelings about being a part of the church.)

AT THE OFFERING

(We asked a mother and her two children to sing some family favorites. They sang two songs and then the mother sang to the children Benjamin Britten's "The Birds.")

READING:
"To Tom McCall, Wherever You Are" (page 37)

(Read by the four Readers)

READING:
"Cough Drops in Church" (page 39)

(Read by a parent and child)

READING:

"I Celebrate Children"

(From "Balloons Belong in Church," page 20. Divide among the four readers the lines beginning with "I celebrate children who laugh out loud" and ending with "And I celebrate adults who are as little children.")

HYMN

(Have the children "teach" the congregation one of their favorite songs.)

SLIDE PRESENTATION: "The Children of the Church"

(Ask that parents bring individual slides of their children to the church about three weeks prior to the service and also make available a church photographer to take pictures of those who do not have slides. You may find it easier just to take slides of all the children and then these can be a gift to the parents at Christmas time or after the service.)

DIALOGUE: "What Do We Want to Tell the Children?"

First Reader: What do we want to tell the children?

Second Reader: We want to tell them that at one time we wandered in darkness. Children know the fears of darkness. But we want to tell them that a man named Jesus Christ came and took our hands and held them tightly so that we would be safe. Children know about holding hands with someone who can make them safe. We want to tell them that this man Jesus led us into the Light and that that's where we live now— in the Light. We want each of our children to know what it means to go from darkness to Light.

First Reader: It's sort of like when nighttime comes and you run upstairs in a hurry because you feel like something will get you and you run as fast as you can and turn on the light and you feel safer. Then you go and find your mother or your daddy or somebody who will put their arms around you and then you *know* you're safe.

Third Reader: That's why adults come to church. They come to be in the Light. And when they come, they realize that there are a lot of people in this world who don't know about the Light of Christ. There are people wandering around in darkness. They're hungry,

and they have people yelling at them all
the time, and they can't do anything
right, and their best friend moves away.
When they do something that they think
is good, nobody bothers to tell them it's
good, and they get sick and nobody cares,
and they don't have a warm bed to sleep
in, and just when they're shivering in the
darkness, somebody comes along and
pushes them, and then they're lying in the
darkness crying.

Fourth Reader: That's why adults come to church. They come
to thank God for the Light, and they go
out into the world and find the people
who are crying in the darkness, and they
pick them up and carry them into the
Light. They wipe away their tears, and
they tell them that they can stay in the
Light, and they hold their hands so they
won't be scared anymore.

First Reader: What do we want to tell the children?

Second Reader: We want to tell them that Jesus calls them to
him and loves them just the way they are.

Fourth Reader: We want to tell them that they are cherished
and that we love them fiercely!

Third Reader: We want to tell them that here in this church
family there's a lot of hand holding going
on because Christ leads us out of darkness
into Light.

HYMN: "Jesus Shall Reign"

*(During the hymn our confirmation class passed out lollipops, in
wicker baskets, to everyone. This symbolized that we are all
children of God. It was a joyful sight watching adults and
children unwrapping and enjoying their lollipops!)*

THE PASSING OF THE PEACE

(Each person greets those around with these words:)

"You are a child of God and God knows your name."

BENEDICTION

Children of God, we affirm your childlikeness, your spontaneity, your wonder, your inquisitiveness, your joy in the abundant life, your humbleness, and your unashamed love of the Lord. Each of you is a child of God, and God knows your name. God knows when you skin your knees or your heart. God knows when you catch a butterfly or cry in the darkness. Go, children, out where the sun shines on your faces. Go out into God's abundance and tell the story of a Christ who would claim each person as a Christian child. Go and kiss the hurts of this world. Go and laugh in the fields of God, for you are Christian children, inheritors of God's grace and love. Amen.

CHORAL PRAYER: "Children of the Heavenly Father"
Swedish melody

(Our choir sang this in Swedish and then the congregation joined them to sing it in English. Words were, of course, available.)

ARE WE CLAPPING
FOR THE WRONG GOD?

CALL TO WORSHIP

"O clap your hands, all you people, shout unto God with the voice of triumph. . . . Sing praises to God, sing praises: sing praises unto our King, sing praises. For God is the King of all the earth: sing praises with understanding. . . . Clap your hands, all you people!" (From Psalm 47)

PROCESSIONAL HYMN: "All Glory, Laud, and Honor"

AFFIRMATION OF FAITH: The Nicene Creed *(or other creed)*

READING OF THE WORD:
                Matthew 7:21–27 from Good News Bible (TEV)

(This is a wonderful Scripture reading that can be easily pantomimed. See if you can find someone in your church or community willing to do this. Find a reader with a strong and dramatic voice.)

DRAMATIC READING: "ARE WE CLAPPING FOR THE WRONG GOD?"

(Three readers are needed. Have them sit on stools in the front of the sanctuary.)

1:          It happened in my house in front of the TV set. A commercial was on. The music started, the singing began, and I found myself professing to believe in—of all things—peanut butter! "If you believe in peanut butter, clap your hands, oh, clap your hands." My ten-year-old son came in one door and out the other saying, "Oh, really, I thought you believed in God."

2:    I believe in one God the Father Almighty, Maker of heaven and earth, and of all things visible and invisible; . . . God of God; Light of Light; Very God of Very God . . .

1:    Don't I? Don't we? We say we do, but are our hands clapping for the wrong god? Who do you say that God is by the way that you live? Could we just as well be clapping for peanut butter? *(pause)*
Good church people:
Not sinners they;

2 and 3:   No-o-o-o!

1:    Not lawbreakers;

2 and 3:   No-o-o-o!

1:    Not thieves;

2 and 3:   No-o-o-o!

1:    Not adulterers;

2 and 3:   No-o-o-o!

1:    But rulemakers,
Upstanding,
Righteous,
Remarkably wonderful church members.

3:    These good church people asked for a Savior—
And when he came,
They knew there had been some mistake.

2:    As long as there were palms to wave
And alleluias to be sung,

134

3:     As long as there were stories told
       And promises of good things to come,

1:     As long as there were loaves and fishes
       And rumors of miracles,

3:     The people danced around him and called him Rabbi.

1:     But when he lived a little too abundantly for their taste
              —for good taste,

2:     When he chose his friends from among ruffians,

1:     Women of the streets,

3:     Tax collectors,

2:     Cursing fishermen,

1:     And then publicly called God his father,
       They knew this wasn't their man.
       So they called him:

3:     Blasphemer,

2:     Lawbreaker,

3:     Sinner-lover.

1:     And they killed him.

(After a pause, have a soloist sing the first verse of the spiritual
       "Were You There When They Crucified My Lord?"*)*

2:     But that was a long time ago.

3:     Hail, hail, the gang's still here.

1:     Today we are the crowd, screaming:
              He's an agitator.
              He's a revolutionary.
              He tells them to love God,
              Yet he breaks the Sabbath laws.
              He tells them to do good,
              Yet he dines with sinners.
              He tells them to love one another

Even when they are wronged.
He tells them to forgive
Even when no pardon is asked.

2:     Today we are Pilates—
       Unable to make a decision,
       Unable to take a stand,
       Unable to risk our pitiful positions,
       Wringing our hands and saying we're not respon-
       sible.

3:     Today we are Sadducees and Pharisees—
       Saying we know how to run this temple, thank
       you!
            Clinging to our written rules,
            Chief among these being:
                 Do not fraternize with the enemy; and
                 Righteous ritual will get you into heaven.

1:     We believe in one God,

2:     The Almighty Dollar, God of the Church Dinner, God
            of the
       Socially Prominent, Father of Fellowship;

1:     And in one Lord Jesus Christ,

3:     Christ of Ceremony, Prince of Programming, Lord of
            Tradition and Correctness, Christ of the Big
            Crowds, Lord of Numbers and Lists, Christ of
            Comfort and Convenience, Lord of our Left-
            overs, King of Busy-Busy.

2:     Are we clapping for the wrong God?

HYMN: "Anybody Listening?"   Avery and Marsh

DIALOGUE: "IS THE CHURCH LISTENING?"

(Take this opportunity to use two other people in your service.)

A: I'm a Christian and I love you.

B: I don't care if you love me; I'm hungry.

A: Well, I do love you.

B: Got any food?

A: Oh, I think we can make some arrangements. Did you hear me say I love you?

B: My stomach can't wait for arrangements.

A: You're not listening to me. I said, "I love you."

B: Yeah, yeah . . . but can you get me a job?

A: We'll put your name on the list. I said, "I love you!"

B: What list?

A: The priority list—but I've just said something very important to you: as a Christian I love you.

B: I don't want to be on a list. I need medicine. I need a place to live. I need friends. And food—oh, how I need food!

A: Look: have faith, be good, and remember we Christians love you.

B: I don't want your love!

A: What do you mean you don't want my love? A wretch like you ought to be grateful!

B: Could you get me a cup of cold water?

A: I love you.

B: Could you get me a cup of cold water?

A: I love you.

B: Could you get me a cup of cold water?

A: I love you.

B: Is anybody listening?

(Someone seated in the congregation comes up to the front, puts an arm around B and leads B away. Then A jumps up and screams the following lines:)

A: What are you going with him (her) for? I said I love you. We Christians love all you people!

(Soloist sings again the first verse of "Were You There When They Crucified My Lord?")

LITANY OF CONFESSION

Minister:

    O God, we have said that we "love" our brothers and our sisters, but we confess it is very difficult to put meaning behind that word.

People:

    We have traded righteousness for success and security, for power, and for popularity.

Minister:

    We have said that we "love" our brothers and sisters but we have not translated that into food and clothing and housing.

People:

    The good that we would do, we do not; and the bad that we would not do, we do.

Minister:

    We have said we love God, but if we do not love our brothers and sisters whom we have seen, how can we love God whom we have not seen?

People:

    We confess that there are times when we do not worship the God of Abraham, but we worship the approval of others, or our own reputations, or our work, or our family, or money. O God, forgive our unfaithfulness. Forgive our following after false gods.

Minister:

O God, there are those who thirst for the Living Water.

People:

We pray that we may be strong enough to come forward with a cup of cold water for our brothers and our sisters.

Minister:

In the name of Christ who ministered unto those in need, we pray.

People:

Amen.

HYMN: "God of Grace and God of Glory"   CWM RHONDDA

OFFERTORY

READING *(continuing the first reading with the same three speakers):*

1:   I believe in one God.

2:   The city is thick with screaming gods. Where is the church?

3:   *(sing-songy)* My church is better than your church.

2:   *(pompous)* I believe in tabling the controversial.

1:   I believe in closed church doors.

3:   All praise to things and correctness.

2:   We say "God," but we mean peanut butter.

1:   Who do we say God is by the way we live? At whose altar are we kneeling? For which god are we clapping?

(At this point in the service have the choir sing or play a recording of the Nicene Creed from the Rejoice Mass. *The congregation is asked to join in as the creed is sung for the second time.)*

BENEDICTION

Go now into the world that God, the Creator, has made for you. Go now and tell the story of the God of God, Light of Light, who for our sake sent Jesus, the Christ, that we might be reconciled to the one true God. Go, believing only in God, the Lord and Giver of Life. Amen.

THIS CUP I GIVE TO YOU

This service was an attempt on the part of the Worship Committee to further the understanding of Communion. Several people had expressed feelings of "missing something" because they did not go from Communion with the sense of spiritual renewal that others felt. This service was the first in a series in which we tried to explain the symbolism of the Eucharist in order to make it real to the families within the church.

For each Communion service a different family is asked to bake the Communion bread. This is a very special act of devotion for these families. For this service we asked that each Communion loaf be marked with a cross and IHS, the first letters of the name "Jesus" in Greek.

We also asked each family unit to bring a cup from their home to be used as a common Communion cup for the family. We emphasized in our church paper prior to the service that a family might be one person or an extended family with grandparents, uncles, aunts, cousins, etc. We also suggested that several single people might want to come as a "family" group and share a common cup. Some families extended invitations to single people to "join" their family for the occasion. We made a point of not excluding anyone, but rather of including everyone as we partook of the bread and wine as the family of God. We also had available in the back of the sanctuary cups for those who may have forgotten theirs or who were visitors that day. Some families brought Dad's coffee cup, familiar to their everyday life; some brought a baby cup, dear to them; some brought cups their grandparents had used; one family brought a cup they had acquired in Jerusalem. Cups of china, silver, plastic, or pottery appeared, representing something special to each family. Whatever the cup, it was never again the same, for we were told by many that their cups had been "set aside" that day. It was a very special dedication.

INTROIT: Improvisation on "Let Us Break Bread Together"

Spiritual

CALL TO CELEBRATION

Minister: Good morning!

People: Good morning!

Minister: We come from many families to worship as one family of God.

People: Remembering our covenant, we come in faithfulness.

Minister: We come to break bread together.

People: We come to receive the cup in Christ's name.

Minister: Come then, let us renew ourselves as we celebrate Holy Communion.

People: *Marana tha*—Our Lord, come!

PROCESSIONAL: "All Hail the Power of Jesus' Name"

CORONATION

RESPONSE   (*Congregation*): "Christ Is Made the Sure Foundation"

REGENT SQUARE

STATEMENT OF MUTUAL COMMITMENT

(Ideally this should be a statement written by a group in your church. If that is not possible, you might want to use the statement on page 17.)

142

THE OFFERING ANTHEM: "They Cast Their Nets in Galilee," from the *Rejoice Mass*

(If there is a family in your church that can sing this anthem, it can be particularly effective. We used guitar accompaniment.)

THE SACRAMENT OF HOLY COMMUNION

INTRODUCTION

(Have a member of the congregation explain the procedure for this Communion service. The congregation should be thanked for bringing their cups and asked to come row by row in family groups to the front of the chancel and to stand around the Communion table. An elder should have been previously appointed to signal to the families as there is room at the table. Several families can, of course, be served Communion at one time. The bread is to be broken and passed with these words: "Christ is the Bread of Life." The family member with the cup brought from home holds the cup to be filled and then passes it to the next person in the family, saying: "This cup I give you in the name of Christ Jesus who died for you." The ministers will repeat these words again each time the bread is passed and the wine is poured.)

* Edie
← start here

THE INVITATION TO THE LORD'S TABLE

Minister:
Friends, we have all been invited to eat supper in the Lord's house.

People:
We come hungry and thirsty.

Minister:
Jesus walked into the world inviting everyone to his feast —the rich and the poor, the faithful and the unfaithful, the strong and the weak, the old and the young, adults and children.

People:

> We meet at the Lord's Table.

Minister:

> Come then and sit down to life with our Lord Jesus Christ,
> for he will wash the dust from your feet—he will wipe
> the tears from your eyes—he will take the burden
> from your shoulders and the heaviness from your
> hearts.

People:

> We come to this table to celebrate life, to celebrate faith.

READING OF THE SCRIPTURE: I Corinthians 11:23–26

HYMN: "Become to Us the Living Bread" O FILII ET FILIAE

COMMUNION LITANY

Minister:

> Jesus was sent by God into the everyday of this world.
> There is nothing more universal than the everyday
> event of sitting down at the table to eat. Bread and
> wine become symbols of life, the life of the Spirit as
> well as the body. Jesus chose these common symbols
> so that everyone would know what he was talking
> about. His life and death are as important to us for
> our spiritual survival as food and drink are for our
> physical survival.

People:

> In his supper he calls us to a communion, a union with him
> and with others. It was scandalous of Jesus to suggest
> that God is interested in our everyday. And yet what
> Jesus meant was that when we eat the bread, repre-
> senting the body of Christ, at the Lord's Table, he is
> enfleshed in us. We are to be faithful to life as he lived
> it. He sat at table with strangers, with prostitutes, tax
> collectors, Pharisees. He calls us, too, to sit down to
> life with strangers, to do justice and to love mercy. He

said he had come to preach good news to the poor, to proclaim release to the captives and recovering of sight to the blind, to set at liberty those who are oppressed, and to proclaim the acceptable year of the Lord.

Minister:

The "acceptable year of the Lord" is a reference to the Old Testament "jubilee year," when everyone was to be made equal. Debts were to be canceled, slaves were to be freed, the land was to be returned to its original owners. The Sabbath is a weekly reminder of this jubilee year. On the Sabbath there are no masters and no slaves, no rich and no poor. There are no strangers. The Sabbath is a weekly reminder of this jubilee year. The Sabbath has to do with whether the whole of life will be created anew.

People:

In the Lord's Supper we are made new persons in Christ, persons who are to be concerned that the Sabbath comes into the lives of all of God's children. When we partake of the bread and the wine, we are remembering that Christ lived and died for us that we might experience the Sabbath. The Lord's Supper is an invitation to all to live life abundantly and to proclaim that death has been overcome. The mission of the church is to help make life more human. We in the church are called, not to make programs, but to sit at table with strangers, to care about what happens to all of God's people.

Minister:

When Jesus took the cup of wine he said, "This cup is God's new covenant sealed with my blood." Long ago God made a covenant, an agreement with the people of this earth: I will be your God and you will be my people. The new covenant speaks of Jesus' sacrifice on the cross. God sent Jesus to live

145

in our everyday. Jesus experienced our humanness. He knew hurt and disappointment and suffering. He even suffered death, the humiliating death of the cross. In his sacrifice for us he entered into our own sense of godforsakenness. In Jesus' resurrection we know that God has overcome death. We then in joyful response seek to enter into and share the suffering of others. The new covenant speaks to the whole idea of the Kingdom of God when the promises will be fulfilled and every day will be the Sabbath. It is that time when the hungry will have bread and every tear will be wiped away.

People:

In the eating of the bread and the drinking of the wine, we are united with one another and with God in the holiest of communions—one that seeks to bring justice and mercy and love to our everyday.

PRAYER OF COMMITMENT AND THE LORD'S PRAYER

Make this a Sabbath moment, O God, as your people come to your table. We especially commend these little children who come to you in innocence. Thank you for our church family. We cherish the love and acceptance that we share here. Keep us close to one another in Christ Jesus. Accept the love we offer and use it to bring in the Kingdom. In the name of him who taught us to pray together: *Our Father, who art in heaven . . .*

HYMN: ~~"Let Us Break Bread Together"~~ Spiritual

Take Our Bread

PRESENTATION OF THE ELEMENTS OF BREAD AND WINE

~~(On this Sunday we ask the family who baked the bread to bring the elements down the aisle.)~~

End

SHARING OF THE BREAD AND CUP

(The elders should assist those coming forward. They should also watch for those families who may be without a cup. Where possible, include single people with a family to receive Communion together. During the Communion time the choir might sing a number of hymns that have Communion themes.)

RESPONSE OF FAITH *(unison)*

God of Jesus Christ, God of this family gathered here, bless us, we pray. We have received the bread and the wine; we are renewed by your Spirit. Go with us as we seek to spread your Spirit in your troubled world. In faith we seek your guidance as we try to flesh out your love. Amen.

HYMN: "The Church's One Foundation"

BENEDICTION

You have supped at the Lord's Table with family; go now to sit among strangers and to tell the story of your Lord. Amen and amen.

HINTS FOR PLANNING WORSHIP

CHOOSING COMMITTEE MEMBERS

Choose people who are willing to put a lot of time into creating a service of worship, people who are willing to study, to learn, and to work. So often we approach people and ask them to help by saying: "It won't take much time." For this committee people should be told it will be difficult and it will take a lot of time. Each member of the committee must be willing to do his or her share.

DISCOVERING YOUR IDENTITY AS A COMMITTEE

Find out who the committee is, in terms of the theology that emerges from a group study.

Suggestions for study:

1. *Studying the Bible*
   a. Matthew 5:23–24
      In what sense can worship give a wholeness to life?
      Why is it important to "make peace" with others before we worship?
   b. John 4:7–26
      What does it mean to worship by the power of God's Spirit?
      What does Jesus mean when he says: "Whoever drinks the water that I will give him will never be thirsty again"?
   c. Colossians 3:15–17

What does this passage say about our worship? our everyday life?

d. Micah 6:6–8

What does the Lord have to say to us about integrating our lives and our worship?

What does the Lord require of us?

e. Matthew 23 and Matthew 6:1–21

Do you see in these passages a warning to church people about being self-righteous?

How can you relate this warning to church people of our day?

What can we do to avoid self-righteousness?

f. Matthew 5:1–16

List the things (in your own words) that Christ says will make people happy.

What list for happiness do you think the average American would make? Compare the two.

How can we "be" the Good News?

2. *Delve into the worship book of your denomination.*
Perhaps you could have someone from the regional worship commission of your denomination come and talk to you. What traditions are important to your denomination in its worship? Where did these originate and why did they become important? What is the traditional order of worship and why is it ordered in this way?

3. *Use the questions below as points of departure for discussion and theologizing.*

a. What attitude do you bring to worship? Are you ready to give as well as to receive? Are you as ready to take responsibility for the service as to be critical of it?

b. Do you think of the words that you hear and repeat as words of witness? Witness to what or whom?

c. Does the order of a worship service effect our concentration and attention? What makes it easy for the mind to wander?

d. How does the worship service affirm your faith?

149

e. Are you willing to learn something new during the worship service? Should you be?
f. Does the service enable you to risk?
g. Is worship an end in itself?
h. What does the worship service say about who you are as a congregation?
i. What portion of the service, if any, is not representative of who you are as a congregation? What portion does not represent who you are personally?
j. How is worship discipleship?
k. In what ways does worship enhance your Christian commitment?
l. What contribution does worship make to your life-style?
m. How does worship affirm the personhood of others?
n. What is the tie between worship and acts of reconciliation, compassion, healing, justice, mercy, and love?
o. When has worship touched you significantly enough to evoke growth and change?
p. Does worship tend to call you away from the pettiness of life?
q. Does worship call attention to the preciousness of the small treasures of life?
r. Is the worship community-centered rather than self-centered?
s. Do you look forward to Holy Communion? What is its meaning to your congregation?
t. In what ways can liturgy be "the people's work"?

These questions can be supplemented with others of your choosing. The value of a study is to bring to the consciousness of this group certain goals that you will want to emphasize in planning worship.

FORMAT FOR PLANNING A WORSHIP SERVICE

1. *Choose a theme.*
   What is the message the committee wants to communicate? Theme suggestions: We're All God's Children; Covenant Relationships; God's World, Our World; How Serious Is

Our Commitment?; Finding Christ in the Carnival;
Where Is Your Treasure?; Beginnings and Endings; Forgiveness.

2. *Elaborate on that theme.*
   Develop the theme from a single thought to a multiple
   concept, or contrast the theme with another theme. For
   instance, the theme "Beginnings and Endings" could
   speak to beginnings and endings in our lives (birth, leaving
   home, broken relationships, marriage, divorce, old age,
   death) and beginnings and endings in nature (spring, sum-
   mer, fall, winter). It could also speak to the great beginnings and endings in the Bible (creation, exodus, advent,
   resurrection).

3. *Decide how the theme can best be interpreted.*
   What means will the committee use to enhance the message, to touch the congregation, to raise consciousness, to
   lead to fulfillment of discipleship? How best do we tell the
   story? The following list suggests some of the ways to help.
   Warning: Don't get gimmicky. Use only those means
   which will point to the message.

dialogue	choral readings	storytelling
drama	litanies	quotations
banners	musical instruments	symbols
dance	visual art	readings
sounds	singing new songs	props
chanting	body banners	cantatas
poetry	calls to worship	body movements
prayer	processionals	pantomime
parades	recessionals	improvisation

4. *Divide the responsibilities.*
   a. Order for the Worship of God: The minister is responsible;
   appoint two or three people to assist in this endeavor.
   b. Choose the means of carrying out the chosen theme: Suppose the full committee has decided to have a choral group
   sit in the chancel area and chant the Scripture, and that
   this Scripture chanting will be interspersed with music and

readings. Someone must choose the appropriate music (include the choir director/organist here) and readings that respond to the message.

c.   Write what there is to be written, if anything. There might be an introduction or a call to worship, or new words to a hymn tune, or a connecting passage bridging two parts of a theme. Perhaps someone will be asked to choreograph an interpretive dance while the choral group is chanting the Scripture. Someone else may be asked to do a piece of visual art, a banner, or a backdrop.

d.   The music must be chosen and appropriate instruments and hymns must be coordinated with the spoken word and fit into the order. The choirmaster and minister would certainly be a part of this group.

e.   Responsibility for the physical setup—props, projector, microphone, lighting, balloons, candles, flowers, and bulletin cover designs would fit into this category.

f.   Choose participants according to their talents, but risk a little. Someone may be hiding his or her talent under a haystack! In general the participants who have speaking parts should read with meaning, with insight, with feeling, with conviction, with a loud, clear voice, and slowly.

g.   Go through the service the preceding week. The committee and participants will need this chance to see that everything falls together. Without a "rehearsal" the service could be sloppy and therefore distracting instead of worshipful. Some people object to practicing a service of worship. But we are not aiming for a perfect "show biz" effect. Rather, we are aiming to be prepared so that the service can be as reverent and meaningful as possible. It is difficult to worship when the microphone is not turned on or someone neglected to get the elements for Communion. Just as the minister and the choir are prepared because they have practiced, participants in the contemporary service of worship must be coordinated and ready for their parts.

h.   Evaluate. Evaluate from the standpoint of trying to discover how the service accomplished the goals the committee had decided upon. Don't berate yourselves for mistakes made. Some are inevitable and much is learned from them. Do evaluate the service from the standpoint of whether the intended message was conveyed. Listen carefully to the remarks of those attending, but don't take every criticism (good or bad) as the gospel truth. Then—happy day!—start getting ready for the next worship service!

i. Have a meeting to look over resources. Ask different members to do some reading, some researching about a particular area of worship or subject theme.

j. Rotate the committee each year to ensure new life in the committee and also to spread worship education among the members of the congregation.

RESOURCES
FOR HYMNS AND ANTHEMS

"All Through the Night" is in many collections, including *Let's Sing Together,* published by The Geneva Press, 925 Chestnut St., Philadelphia, Pa. 19107.

Avery and Marsh songs—"Thank You, Lord," "Come as a Little Child," "Sing Love Songs," and "Hey! Hey! Anybody Listening?" can be found in *The Avery and Marsh Songbook,* published by Proclamation Productions, Inc., Orange Square, Port Jervis, N.Y. 12771.

"Children of the Heavenly Father" is published as an anthem by Augsburg Publishing House, 426 South 5th St., Minneapolis, Minn. 55415.

"Everything Is Beautiful" can be found in music stores. The record is published by Ahab Productions and distributed by CBS, Inc., 51 West 52nd St., New York, N.Y. 10019.

Godspell songs—"Day by Day" and "Save the People"—are popular and can be found in music stores, libraries, and religious bookstores. Sheet music is available from New Cadenza Music Corp., 1650 Broadway, New York, N.Y. 10019. The record is available from Bell Records, Columbia Pictures, Inc., 1776 Broadway, New York, N.Y. 10019. "Day by Day" is also in *The Genesis Songbook,* published by Agape, Main Place, Carol Stream, Ill. 60187.

Joseph and the Amazing Technicolor Dreamcoat can be found in religious bookstores. It is also available from Belwin Mills Publishing Corp., Rockville Centre, N.Y. 11571.

"Morning Has Broken" is in *The Genesis Songbook;* also in *The Hymnbook,* published by The Westminster Press.

"O Lamb of God" *(Agnus Dei)* can be found in most hymnbooks. Or ask your director of music, who can find a setting of these words. Also in *The Genesis Songbook* and in the *Rejoice Mass* (see below).

"Pass It On" is included in *Tell It Like It Is,* available from Sacred Songs, Box 1790, Waco, Tex. 76703. Also in *Creation Sings,* published by The Geneva Press (address given above).

Rejoice Mass hymns—"O Lamb of God" *(Agnus Dei),* "Sanctus," and "They Cast Their Nets"—were written by Herbert G. Draesel and are available from Marks Music Corp., 136 West 52nd St., New York, N.Y. 10019. The record is available from Scepter Records, Inc., 254 West 54th St., New York, N.Y. 10019.

Spirituals are included in many hymnbooks and in various collections. Here are some specific sources: (1) *The Books of American Negro Spirituals* (two vols. in one), ed. by James Weldon Johnson and J. Rosamond Johnson; Da Capo Press, Inc., 227 West 17th St., New York, N.Y. 10011; (2) *The Contemporary Hymnbook,* David Yantis Publications, 1505 47th St., San Diego, Calif. 92102; (3) *Let's Sing Together;* and (4) *Maranatha Song Book,* Maranatha Publications, P.O. Box 672, Saratoga, Calif. 95070.

Most of the other hymns suggested can be found in many hymnbooks. Two in particular—"The Day of Pentecost Arrived" and "The Lone, Wild Bird"—will be found in *The Worshipbook— Services and Hymns,* published by The Westminster Press, 925 Chestnut St., Philadelphia, Pa. 19107.

BIBLIOGRAPHY

For the reader who is interested in further study or resources, I suggest the following:

Brown, Robert McAfee. *Frontiers for the Church Today.* Oxford University Press, 1973.

Keen, Sam. *To a Dancing God.* Harper & Row, 1970.

Kent, Corita. *Footnotes and Headlines.* Herder & Herder, 1967.

Killinger, John. *Leave It to the Spirit.* Harper & Row, 1971.

Raines, Robert. *Creative Brooding.* Macmillan Co., 1966.

Rivers, Clarence Joseph. *Celebration.* Herder & Herder, 1969.

White, James F. *New Forms of Worship.* Abingdon Press, 1971.